JACKIE STORER

Historical Consultant: Dr Stephen Bull

HIDDEN STORIES OF THE FIRST WORLD WAR

THE BRITISH LIBRARY

For Dad, whose love and advice I miss every day, and to my darling husband Chris Jones and our gorgeous girls – Jasmine, Edie and Ellen – I couldn't have done this without you.

First published in 2014 by
The British Library
96 Euston Road
London NW1 2DB

europeana
1914-1918

in association with Europeana
1914–1918

© 2014 Jackie Storer

British Library Cataloguing in
Publication Data
A CIP Record for this book is
available from the British Library
ISBN 978 0 7123 5738 8

Edited by Mark Hawkins-Dady
Designed by Andrew Barron
Printed by Gutenberg Press, Malta

The vast majority of
illustrations in this book were
generously provided by the
families of the subjects directly
or via Europeana 1914–1918
or Great War Archive.
In addition, the publishers
are grateful to the following
for permission to use images:
Stephen Bull (p. 31); Cleveland
Press Collection (p. 90);
Imperial War Museums:
HU66128 (p. 66), Q39007
(p. 68), Q60549 (p. 110),
Q79589 (p. 128), CO3373
(p. 173); Library and Archives
Canada (p. 116); Orkney
Library and Archive (pp. 39,
40, 118); Wikimedia (p. 151).

Foreword

The battlefields of the First World War have disappeared, but isolated remnants can still be seen, in the form of craters and short strips of trench, polished into softness by a hundred years of rain and spring floods. The men who fought there are also gone now. So the landscapes of the cataclysm have finally been turned over to all of us who weren't there and who can't know them as they were. Time moves on, and distance increases, inexorably.

It is both for better and for worse. The passions that once made the Great War possible have ebbed away. This allows for a more reasoned understanding, which was difficult and perhaps even impossible before. But there is a complication here. When the past is turned into history, part of the complexity invariably gets lost, not least because of the overwhelming need to mould a confusing and chaotic reality into a neat and tidy narrative. In this process, individuals can become – at best – small specks of light flickering by, to prove a point or lend some colour.

What Frederic Manning called the 'mystery' of war still haunts us. Perhaps it always will. But part of our own understanding of this supremely important historical event surely must come from trying to understand the individuals that were part of it and the multiplicity of their experiences and feelings. This book adds to that understanding and does so in a beautiful way, not least by showing that for individual participants and for those left behind, war isn't over just because the battlefields fall silent.

Peter Englund

Contents

AUTHOR'S NOTE

The First World War – the 'Great War' – shocked people at the time. It still has the power to do so, a hundred years later. It was unprecedented in its intensity and violence, its human and material cost, and its global scale. It extinguished three empires, redrew the maps of three continents, and brought about Bolshevik and German revolutions. It saw the beginnings of American superpowerdom and – depending on whom you listen to – sowed the seeds of fascism, appeasement, another world war, and a Cold War to boot.

Yet beneath all the geopolitical and strategic significance, it was also a war of personal experience – of the ordinary civilian and serviceman on the home and fighting fronts. This was an inescapable war, in which whole societies had to be mobilised in a way they had not been before. Men who had never contemplated violence were conscripted into it; women who had never imagined themselves manufacturing explosives or digging the land were doing just that; children who just wanted to play went hungry, were bombed from the air, and became orphans. Many people today can therefore trace back a generation or two to find a direct ancestral involvement in the war. Perhaps for these reasons, personal testimony has proved a particularly durable route towards understanding what happened in 1914–18.

Hidden Stories of the First World War continues that tradition by presenting 32 newly revealed and diverse encounters with events. The majority have their genesis in the recent Europeana 1914–1918 project, which, through its roadshows, has encouraged people across Europe to share their families' histories and artefacts, preserving this documentary evidence for future generations through its ambitious digitisation programme. The 32 stories move broadly chronologically, from the trepidations of a French pacifist in August 1914 to a lucky Welsh survivor of the last weeks of fighting in 1918. In between, they range across nationalities and borders, land and sea, home front and fighting front, social class, life and death, drama and quietude, high seriousness and unexpected humour. Throughout, individuals find themselves caught up in the fates of people and places that, for good or ill, have resonated since – Lord Kitchener, Ypres, the Somme, Passchendaele, Verdun, even the young Adolf Hitler.

Yet, highly diverse and contrasting though these stories are, themes emerge that suggest a commonality of experience, too. In a war where so many men simply vanished and were described as 'missing' (in part a terrible acknowledgement that the modern battlefield obliterated the human body), the unexpected return of loved ones presumed dead turns out to be one such theme. For most, despite the dislocations of war, life went on after 1918. These stories are about the Great War; but they are about its afterlife too – about how the survivors, their children (and grandchildren) came to terms with the impact of the 'war to end all wars'.

Acknowledgements

This book could not have been written without the Europeana 1914–1918 project and its online treasure trove of stories and pictures. Thanks to Executive Director Jill Cousins, Ad Pollé, Jon Purday and the Europeana team, I was able to attend many of their roadshows and hear the stories first-hand from relatives and descendants. I am also immensely grateful to Oxford University's IT Services Department, whose Great War Archive started the whole 'crowd-sourcing' project. Particular thanks go to Oxford's Dr Ylva Berglund Prytz, Alun Edwards, Dr Stuart Lee and Kate Lindsay, who not only drew my attention to some of the best stories and unearthed photographs but also became good friends during our many European excursions together.

Another friend and constant source of expertise, wise counsel and patience throughout the writing and research process has been Dr Stephen Bull. The historical context of the stories has been improved immeasurably by his attention to detail and encyclopaedic knowledge of all things related to the First World War. I also appreciate the help I've received from many other historians, including Everett Sharp, Frank Drauschke, Dr Thomas Weber, Jørgen Gram Christensen, Dominiek Dendooven, Roger V. Verbeke, Eric Rombouts and Brian Budge.

I'm indebted to the translators who helped me interview family members during my trips overseas or transcribed foreign text when I returned home, especially Freddy Rottey, Fabiana Rosat, Hannelore Akkermans, Marion Ansel, Bruno Sagna, Karmen Štular Sotošek, Constanze Seifert and Natacha Robert; and to the many museums and their staff who made me so welcome, including: Annick Vandenbilcke, Sophie Serraris, Valeria Balassone and Federica Pellegatti. Thank you to Buckinghamshire County Museum, David Baynham at the Royal Regiment of Fusiliers Museum, John Hardcastle at Scapa Flow Visitor Centre, and to *The New York Times*, *The Huntsville Daily Times* and The Cleveland Press Collection. Thanks also to Michael Cross, Jacky Pinnock, John Stark Bellamy II, Patrick Fleming, Mikkel Christoffersen, Aubéry Escande, and John and Sheila Jones: you all know how you helped, and I'll be forever grateful.

Fundamentally, it is the personal accounts of the individuals who experienced the First World War that have made this book possible. To them and to the family members who keep those experiences alive (and whose names are mentioned in the 32 stories) I owe the biggest debt of thanks. In particular, I'd like to mention those descendants who went the extra mile to answer my many questions. They include: Jillian Scott, Els Deroo, Ghislain Cornette, Louis Van Gysel, Anna Maria Van Humbeeck, Leslie Morey, Katherine Cooperstein, Joan Almond, John Stafford, Simon Ray, Michael Andrews, Tom Muir, Yohann Le Tallec, Florence Groshens, Una Barrie, Vincenzo Cali, Maureen Rogers, Elizabeth Richards, Brian Blennerhassett, Denis O'Neill, Don Mullan, Carl Mullan, Stephen and Sylvia Hurst, Kathleen and Stan Stewart, Francine Fuqua, Marjorie Manson and Valerie Richards.

Jackie Storer, March 2014

DÉPARTEMENT DE L'OISE

CANTON DE *Nanteuil*

Commune
de *Rozières*

Signalement

Age: *22 ans*
Taille *1 m 68*
Cheveux *châtains*
Sourcils *..*
Barbe *....*
Yeux *gris*
Nez *moyen*
Menton *rond*
Front *large*
Teint *pâle*
Signes particuliers
néant

Signature du titulaire :

M Donzé

CARTE D'IDENTITÉ

Enregistrée sous le n° *14* permettant au titulaire de circuler librement (1) dans les limites de la commune et dans le périmètre suivant (indiquer les communes limitrophes ou le canton et les cantons limitrophes) : *Nanteuil le Haudouin, Senlis, Crépy en Valois Betz, Dammartin, Pont St Maxence*

Je soussigné, Maire de la commune de *Rozières* délivre la présente carte d'identité à Madame *Donzé Marie née Salettes* (nom et prénoms)
Profession de *Infirmière*
De nationalité (2) *Française*
Domicilié dans ma commune *Rozières par Nanteuil le Haudouin* (adresse exacte)
Depuis le *15 Mars 1915*

Je certifie qu'à ma connaissance, son attitude au point de vue national n'a jamais donné lieu à remarque.

Fait à *Rozières*, le *10 Octobre* 1916

Le Maire (3),

A Molaye

En cas de perte de la présente carte d'identité, aviser la gendarmerie la plus voisine

(*Voir au verso pour les renvois*)

SENLIS. — IMP. E. VIGNON FILS.

'Damn the war'
A PACIFIST ON THE FRONT LINE

Twenty-six-year-old Edouard 'Emile' Donzé was strongly opposed to the First World War. Unusually for the head of a bank – the Belfort branch of the Crédit Lyonnais in eastern France – he was a committed socialist, who used every influence he had to prevent the war. According to his great-grandson, he took advantage of his close links with Jean Jaurès, the leader of the socialist movement in France, and wrote copious letters to likeminded comrades in Germany, appealing for their help to campaign for a peaceful solution. Jaurès – leader of SFIO, the French Section of the Workers' International – was organising strikes in France and Germany in the hope it would force the governments to negotiate. Both attempts ended in failure. Jaurès was assassinated on 31 July 1914 by a pro-war French nationalist, and that same day Emile was conscripted into the French army.

On 3 August, Germany declared war on France. For Emile Donzé, who was born on 11 September 1887 and grew up in Perouse, a small village near Belfort on the German border, the outbreak of hostilities was a personal tragedy. His young wife Marie, a primary schoolteacher, had recently given birth to their first child, a daughter called Marguerite – and as banking was not a reserved occupation in France, he knew he would be sent to war. Emile soon found himself serving as a sergeant in the 35th Infantry Regiment based in Belfort, and he was permitted to stay with Marie until he received orders to move.

In a letter to his wife's sister, Guite, the day before he was conscripted, Emile described how war fever had swept through the region and expressed his concerns for his young family. 'For the past four days we've been getting more and more nervous. Marie tried to enlist with the Red Cross, but when we thought about our young daughter, we decided to wait for the official call to arms before sending the two of them away from the city. Up until now, Marie has been very brave, but this evening she couldn't stop crying. If you could see Belfort today, you would see a

◀

MARIE DONZÉ'S IDENTITY CARD, ISSUED IN OCTOBER 1916, SHOWS SHE WAS 22
WHEN SHE REGISTERED AS A NURSE A YEAR EARLIER.

town overcrowded with soldiers – infantrymen, cavalry men and artillerymen – moving continuously towards the border. Brawls have arisen in front of banks like mine, as people try to get their money out of their accounts. You should see the crowds of civilians fleeing the villages near the border. Believe me; I'd prefer a war in comparison with this state of uncertainty. Here, everybody thinks that the outbreak of war is just a matter of hours, maybe minutes, away. Nevertheless, everyone is ready to do his duty. Our hearts are ready – you can hardly see any signs of weakness. If you could see how calm our young soldiers are, moving towards the frontier. A few minutes ago, we received news that a skirmish occurred between French and German soldiers near the villages of Chavannes and Montreux. The Germans have destroyed the rail line just ahead of Montreux. The 6.30 train this evening was cancelled. I can hardly explain to you what I am seeing ... I strongly believe that in our century war should not exist. But what's the point of having ideals like these? Following the order of one single man, millions of people are about to cut each other's throats. Yes, the European war which is coming is a shame! To avoid this bloodshed, it is so important that the socialist theories come to reality within all European states.'

Emile's attentions then turned to his wife. 'Marie is by me – she is getting more and more nervous as she thinks she can hear the noise of the guns. If I have to leave her and my young daughter, I will do my duty without any thoughts of hate or revenge. Dear Guite, we have to face this terrible reality. Maybe tomorrow I will cross the frontier. If I fall, please guide my young wife through life – help her as she is too young to live by herself. Maybe in a few days we will meet again. It will be the time to forget this nightmare.' Under Emile's signature, a heartbroken Marie added: 'I can write no more. I have too much sorrow in my heart. This nightmare is awful. I'm sick. All day long I can see young soldiers moving to the frontier. Tomorrow, I will receive my wage and the company will close. I have bought some socks for Emile. I don't know where my beloved will be when you receive this letter. I can't live without him. I pray to find a solution. If something happens, I don't want to leave Belfort because, even beyond his death, my husband would need my presence. If only you could feel the atmosphere here; the sorrow, the fear. I can't believe if he has to leave I will never see him again. I love you all so much.'

Within days of writing this letter, and now in the army, Emile and his comrades from the 35th Infantry Regiment were moved over the border. For France, the war had presented a perfect opportunity to seize back the region of Alsace, which

EMILE DONZÉ IN UNIFORM:
DESPITE OPPOSING THE WAR, HE FOUGHT WITH THE 35TH INFANTRY REGIMENT.

France had been forced to cede to the new German Empire after defeat in the Franco-Prussian War (1870–1).[1] On 6 August Emile described to Marie some of the scenes that took place in the hours leading up to France's opening salvo of the war – the Battle of Mulhouse. 'My beloved wife, I'm near Altkirch [a border town near Mulhouse]. Quite a few of my comrades fell during the battle. The French artillery is far better than the German artillery – even though we've suffered heavy losses. What is unbelievable is there are no class distinctions between us – even between a peasant and someone like me, the head of a bank. I hope that I will come back to tell you how brave we were during these battles.'

On 7 August, French troops crossed the frontier and seized Altkirch with a bayonet charge. The advance continued, and the following day they took Mulhouse, an important industrial base on the Rhine. The success sparked widespread celebrations across France, and the soldiers who arrived in the city were treated as liberators. However, their happiness was short-lived. Emboldened by the arrival of more reserves, the Germans mounted a counter-attack on 9 August, compelling the French to withdraw to their starting lines near Belfort. But on 13 August, a second French offensive was ordered. Emile told his wife how pleased the people of Mulhouse had been to see them and expressed his hope that he would return home soon. His letter dated 14 August 1914 says: 'As you can see, I haven't been killed yet and I hope to keep safe. I'm always thinking about you and our little darling, Marguerite. This is the second time I've been in battle – once in Burnhaupt and once a bit after Mulhouse, last Sunday. I have been on the front line from 4pm to 5am. We have had quite a few losses, but the Germans [no capital letter for 'German' showing a lack of respect] more than us. Yesterday, there was a fight on my right which I wasn't part of. Our artillery was fabulous, delivering heavy losses on the German army. I don't want to give you any more details as war is awful. The city of Mulhouse received us with enthusiasm; people were throwing flowers, they gave us food, drinks and tobacco. I am not in Mulhouse any more. This letter is sent to you from a field between Vauthiermont (French) and Bellemagny (German). I wrote a letter yesterday, but I had to destroy it on the battlefield because we were surrounded

COLLAR PATCH FROM EMILE'S UNIFORM BEARING THE REGIMENTAL NUMBER '35', AND A SMALL PAPER FLAG, AS SENT TO MARIE AFTER HIS DEATH IN 1914.

by German soldiers and I would have been compromised if I'd been wounded. My love, I like you very much – you and my little daughter know it. I love you all, as well as our old Guite, daddy and mummy. Tell me what life has been like since we parted. What is our little darling doing and also what are the papers saying? We don't know anything here. I am starting to be tired. We are sleeping in fields, forests and we are eating when we can. But don't worry about me – take care of you and our little kid. I will make up this time when I get home. I'll be so happy when I see you all again. Don't worry if you don't receive news for a long time as it is not easy – but write to me often ... Talk to you soon my dear love and my little darling. Lots of kisses to mum, dad and our old Guite. Emile.'

Despite Emile's upbeat message home, the second attempt to reclaim Mulhouse on 19 August ended in failure. At the same time, the German army was successfully crossing Belgium towards Paris, threatening the French capital and northern France. Joseph Joffre, the French commander-in-chief, was forced to draw a halt to the Alsace offensive and instead focus his efforts on redirecting some units towards Amiens, to meet this German threat. A whole new army – the Sixth – was created, and on 28 August the 7th Corps, to which Emile belonged, was transferred by train to join the ranks as they gathered near Amiens to defend the Somme and the Aisne rivers.

Before leaving the Alsace region, Emile wrote to his wife (23 August) to tell her that despite his unit suffering heavy losses, he believed the Germans were on the back foot. While he hoped to return uninjured, he gave Marie instructions on whom to contact should he die. He added: 'Yesterday I received a letter and postcard from you – they are the first ones – and you can imagine how happy I was. Despite not receiving them all, I beg you to write to me often. Your letters help me during hard times. I will read them again to enhance my courage. We are already far into Germany (Alsace). The boches [i.e. Germans] don't have our bravery; they are scared of our cannons and bayonets. I hope to come back. I want it for you and our child – then I will tell you all about the beautiful prowess of our soldiers. Three days ago, in a fabulous battle, we took 30 cannons, made 1,000 soldiers prisoner and thousands of Germans are buried under the battlefield. We cried over the loss of very good friends who fell around us. Finally we won and the French flag is everywhere. You will be very proud of me when I tell you about the terrible days I've been through. Don't be sad, lovely. Take good care of yourself. I love you; you are everything for me with my little darling. Big hugs; kisses for her and for daddy. We have just received orders to leave for the front again. I will write as soon as I have a spare moment.'

As the German advance was faster than expected, with some of their troops reaching within 30 miles of Paris, the French Sixth Army had to retreat south of the River Marne. On 6 September, it attacked a flank of the German First Army on the River Ourcq, opening up a sizeable gap which was exploited by the Tommies of the British Expeditionary Force and the French Fifth Army. Over the next two days, the French Sixth Army was reinforced by 6,000 reserve infantrymen from Paris – transported to the battlefield by taxi cab.[2] On 8 September, the French Fifth Army launched a surprise attack on the German Second Army, further widening the gap. In a letter written at 8am on 9 September, Emile told Marie how hard the battle had been: 'My beloved wife, we are completely exhausted. Most of my comrades have died, but we have to make this step to save France. We are working with English troops and we're preparing an assault for the end of this morning. Things are terrible – I can't explain to you the savagery of this war. I hope that I can come back and see you very soon, but just keep in mind that you can be proud of your husband. I think about my young daughter all the time, but I'm sure I will see her very soon. What a pity that with my great ideas about mankind I wasn't able to prevent such a catastrophe. But I am sure that we'll save France against the German emperor. I can't write more because we're being called by the officers and we're moving to the front line. If you can, just write to me and kiss my young daughter one more time. Emile Donzé.'

According to his great-grandson, Yohann Le Tallec, this was his last message home. Emile was hit by an artillery shell and died at 10am that same day – just two hours after he wrote his letter, and just two days before his 27th birthday. He was buried where he fell, in the small town of Chèvreville, north-east of Paris. The Battle of Marne – dubbed the 'Miracle of the Marne' – was an important Allied victory, which ended with the Germans falling back to an area north of the Aisne, where they dug in. The years of trench warfare were about to begin. However, it had been a costly battle too, resulting in 250,000 French soldiers being killed, wounded or captured, with a similar number of German troops suffering the same fate and the loss of almost 13,000 men from the much smaller BEF contingent.

Marie was only informed of her husband's death by the French military administration on 20 December 1914 – more than three months later – and was sent the sum total of his belongings: some ripped pieces of his uniform, including his collar patch with the number '35' referring to his regiment. The couple, who wed in 1908 when Marie was just 16-years-old, had only been together a short time. It is likely that the young widow tried to take comfort in Emile's letters home, because on one he sent to Guite on 30 July 1914 she scribbled: 'Letter from Emile to my sister the day before the declaration of war. Emile, dead gloriously the 9 September at Chèvreville. Damn the war.' Unable to settle after his death, Marie decided to join the nursing corps in March 1915, aged twenty-two. She left her baby daughter in the care of her father, Marius, and served on the front line until her death in 1917 from Spanish flu, the pandemic that would claim more lives than the war itself. 'I can only assume Marie felt totally lost when she found out about Emile's death,' said Yohann. 'She was no more than a child herself when they married, so she was used to having Emile look after her. It's clear from their letters how they felt about each other. I imagine becoming a nurse on the front line was her way of staying close to him.'

The couple's daughter Marguerite grew up in Montluçon, central France, living with her grandfather Marius, a former docker in Marseille who helped build the Orient Express railway. As an adult, Marguerite followed in her mother's footsteps and became a teacher; however, she was her father's daughter and inherited many of his socialist ideals. According to her grandson, Yohann, she was a pacifist who initiated the socialist movement in France during the 1930s. 'She joined the resistance movement in France during the Second World War and concealed Jewish children in her class – even throwing the list of pupils into a heater to burn when the French police arrived,' he said. 'Like many families, she was obliged to host German soldiers in her own home, while at the same time she was hiding two young Jews there, in addition to bringing up her own three children. In the 1950s she was honoured by the Israeli government as one of the thousands of people who risked their lives to save Jews in Nazi Europe. She was quite a character, and often talked to me about her parents. She never felt abandoned by them, just proud of what they did.'

Endnotes

1 Alsace, on France's eastern border and on the west bank of the Upper Rhine, was a constant subject of Franco-German dispute in the 19th and 20th centuries. After the Treaty of Versailles (1919), it returned to French possession.

2 As the German forces closed in on the French capital, the French military authorities called for these emergency troop reinforcements from Paris, and to speed up their dispatch, the fleet of Paris taxis was requisitioned to transport them to the front. The so-called 'Taxis of the Marne' assumed legendary status.

'An Alsatian from France'
FIGHTING FOR THE ENEMY

Henry Groshens was a family man, and a patriotic one too. The only child of laundry worker and single mother Emilie Groshens, he was born in the farming community of Rothau in Alsace – the disputed region that had been lost to the newly unified Germany in 1871, after France's mauling in the Franco-Prussian War. Henry worked hard as a shop assistant in the local hardware store 'Lehr et Loux', selling kitchen utensils, nails and other household goods. He had been there since he was 13 years old and had virtually grown up with his boss's sons and daughters, becoming particularly close to Louise Lehr, the second of the three girls, who was a sweet-natured, talented seamstress and cook. Despite being complete opposites – he very proud and serious, while she was kind and patient (and very religious) – the pair fell in love.

Henry was fiercely loyal to his region; and, despite German control of Alsace, he

always considered himself a Frenchman. When Germany declared war on France in August 1914, Henry, then aged 23, was therefore devastated to be conscripted into the German army. 'It was not what he wanted – he had no choice – and it was an episode of his life that made him deeply ashamed,' his grand-daughter commented a century later. However, Henry did what was asked of him. He went for military training in Weimar, in

◀

HENRY GROSHENS (*CENTRE*)
AS A VERY RELUCTANT GERMAN SOLDIER,
AT WEIMAR, OCTOBER 1914.

September 1914, before being sent to Belgium, where he served in the 7th Company of the 236th Reserve Infantry Regiment during their time in Brussels, Ghent, Roeselare and Rumbeke.[1]

On 20 April 1915 – just two days before the start of the Second Battle of Ypres, which notoriously saw the Germans use poison gas for the first time on the Western Front – Henry expressed his disquiet about being a 'German' soldier and mocked the censors who had returned two of his postcards because they were written in French. In a letter home, penned in German from Hooglede, he recorded: 'We are four days away from Rumbeke and I've had no time to write to you. We've been in the trenches for two days and three nights ... On my last day at Rumbeke I received the two cards I'd sent you – one to Hélène [Louise's cousin] and the other to Louise. The two cards were returned by the company, with a remark from the chief: "As a German soldier, you should be ashamed of yourself, writing a French card, etc., etc." I do feel ashamed to write in German, but I am proud to be an Alsatian and for being punished for being French. I only wish those pen pushers who get the Iron Cross could spend two weeks in the trenches saving their homeland ... .' And in an act of defiance, he signs off in French: 'Merci, very much. Greetings, Henry.'

By late April, Henry was in St Julien, four miles north of Ypres, and it is quite possible that he was involved in the Germans' second gas attack, on the 24th, this time against Canadian troops, which resulted in more than 3,000 Canadian casualties. The battle had a profound effect on Henry, who later told his family that he had witnessed 'sheer butchery'. In one short letter from St Julien, dated 28 April, he told Louise: 'What we have lived through during these past few days is more horrible than I can say. I am safe and sound, but nine men from our company are no longer with us. Best kisses to all, Your Henry.'

While Henry's regiment was moved on to other locations in occupied Belgium – Langemarck, Lichtervelde, Halluin and Ostend – Louise tried to keep his spirits up by sending copious love letters to remind him of better times. In one letter, sent on 19 July 1915, she told him that the soldiers in Rothau were happy and never tired of playing the accordion, adding: 'Oh, my dear Henry, it reminds me of the night we were in the hotel garden. Do you remember? You taught me to dance. How I would like to be in your arms again and to hear your words again because they feel so good. When I think about you, I can't suppress my tears. I wonder where you are. If only you had leave! I keep dreaming that you are back. The reality would be better than this dream. We hope that this will be sooner rather than later. I'm glad I didn't finish my letter this morning – I had the feeling something would arrive for me, and when Michel brought me your little card of July 14, it made me doubly happy. I always feel happy when I get something from you. When I receive your letters; the whole of my body trembles. Oh you are so good for me. I can never tell you often enough. I have to finish this letter, but what can I send you? At least a thousand good kisses – I will be so happy when I can kiss you once more. Your one true love, Louise, who loves you with every fibre of her being. A thousand kisses from your Lou.'

According to his grand-daughter Florence, Henry had seen too much bloodshed by this time and there was nothing Louise or anyone else could say that would make him feel better. 'At one point, the brain of one of his friends landed in his lap,' she said. 'He didn't want to be a German soldier, and seeing the carnage during that battle, he knew he had to do something drastic and get away, which is what he and his friend did, eventually. We only discovered what happened when we found my grandfather's [1927] application for the *Médaille des Évadés* [Medal for Escaped Prisoners of War] and the *Croix de Guerre*.'[2] In this, Henry wrote: 'On the night of August 23 to 24, 1915, my friend Jacques Kuehn of Ammerschwihr, near Colmar, and I succeeded in getting out of the German trenches in the presence of an NCO, by pleading that we had received orders to tighten the barbed wire.' In a separate but similar account, his friend Jacques added: 'After crawling all night long between the trenches, almost encountering German patrols several times, we arrived about 60 metres from the English trenches at 6am, as the fog began to dissipate. (The distance between the opposing trenches was about 500 metres at this point.) As we lay down to make signals with fabric bandage, two machine guns and all the rifles started firing at us. When the shooting stopped, we began our signals again, but immediately the firing started with more intensity. On the other side, the Germans were put on alert and began firing in our direction, so we were being fired at from both sides. Finally, after a third attempt at signalling, and because we screamed with all our might the word "Alsatian", the English stopped firing and signalled to us to come towards them.' In his recollections, Henry said: 'The English regiment that welcomed us was called, if I remember correctly, "Leicester". I was then visited by several English officers to whom I gave, with great pleasure, information about fortifications and battalions in the German sector.'

▶

HENRY IN THE EXOTIC UNIFORM OF A ZOUAVE, AND NOW FIGHTING FOR THE ALLIES, 1915.

HENRY AND LOUISE GROSHENS,
IN HAPPIER TIMES.

Just days after their escape, on 1 September 1915, Henry volunteered to join the French Foreign Legion, but was instead assigned to the 3rd Zouaves, a light infantry regiment originally recruited from France's North African colonies of Algeria and Tunisia. [3] He was sent to Constantine (a city in Algeria), and then to Nam Dinh in French Indo-China (now in Vietnam) in 1916 as a Private First Class. He was later promoted corporal and attached to the 4th Tonkinese Rifles, another Indo-Chinese light infantry corps. [4] He returned home on 9 October 1919.

In a letter dated 24 November 1918, and written in French, Louise told Henry of her happiness at seeing the arrival of French soldiers in Rothau on the 17th of that month and how she could not wait to see him again. 'Rothau was decked out – you should have seen how everyone did their best to receive them. I had the chance to talk to several of these soldiers who were so touched by the reception they had. We all would have liked to have done more, but they said seeing how happy we were made them happy and that was a reward in itself. The colonel also arrived. How good it would have been if you'd suddenly stepped out of the ranks, but we knew that was not possible, given the distance that separates us. I think and hope that you'll do your best to get home quickly. Are we really going to have that happy reunion after five years of separation?'

A year after they were reunited, Henry and Louise were married, and the couple went on to have two children – Emmy Lutz and Jean-Claude Groshens. While Henry made a successful career at the tyre manufacturers Bergougnan – rivals to Michelin – he quickly discovered that his escape from the German army had made him a marked man. 'A German comrade told him after the war that when their commandant had discovered he and Jacques were missing, he was furious,' said grand-daughter Florence. 'He punished the NCO publicly in front of every soldier, and Jacques and my granddad were condemned to death by the German army for their escape. The threat, and the fact he had served in the German army, caused my grandfather so much trouble during the Second World War, he changed the family name – temporarily – to Bergougnan, the company he worked for.'

Henry and Louise were married for more than half a century before she died in 1974. 'In the months after her death, my grandfather seemed completely lost,' said Florence. 'She was so caring and attentive – I know he felt guilty that he wasn't as kind to her as he should have been. But in the depths of his grief, my granddad met another woman, who to our great surprise was a Catholic. The relationship showed that despite being an old man, he still had a rebellious streak. However, to me, he will always be remembered as a secretive and mysterious man, who only gave away snippets of information to my parents. He was 93 when he died in 1984 – I only discovered the true extent of his involvement in the war when I found this archive of letters and documents after my father's death in 2010. It was then I understood how deeply hurt he felt about his dual life: officially born German, yet living as "an Alsatian from France" and speaking French and German. Somehow he managed to overcome that personal conflict to rebuild his life and we are very proud of him.'

Endnotes

1 The Reserve Infantry Regiment No. 236 was raised in the Prussian Rhineland and made up of 'Ersatz' Reservists and volunteers. It was part of the 51st Reserve Division, 102nd Reserve Brigade and went into action north-east of Ypres in mid October 1914; it was one of the so-called 'young regiments', which suffered heavily near Langemarck.

2 The Médaille des Évadés was awarded by the French government to French POWs who escaped during the First World War, but also to citizens of Alsace and Lorraine who deserted from the German army to enlist in the French forces, or to civilians who were interned in Germany but who crossed enemy lines to make themselves available to the French military authorities. The Croix de Guerre was awarded to all those mentioned in dispatches from the outbreak of war. Henry Groshens had a Silver Star emblem, for mention at division level.

3 The Zouaves' usual, colourful uniforms had more in common with the lands of their origin than the Western Front. During the war the Zoaves were expanded to nine regiments and forced to adopt khaki combat uniforms; but they retained their dashing reputation in the attack.

4 The Tonkinese Rifles were led by French officers, many of whom were recalled to the Western Front in the First World War.

'The eggs were laid'
THE SINKING OF *HMS AUDACIOUS*

As Rudolf Kämmerer peered through the darkness on board the German liner *Berlin*, 200 mines were dropped quietly into the Irish Sea. On most of the devices, the *Berlin*'s crew had scrawled anti-British sentiments in chalk, saying they were gifts for 'cowardly Brits' and 'decorated mines to make you pay for your crimes'. There was even a mine for the British Foreign Secretary Edward Grey: 'For our friend Grey, we bring for Christmas an Easter egg.' [1] Rudolf joked, in his account of their clandestine operation, that the slogans proved 'the Germans had never lost their sense of humour', adding they were merely 'verses and loving wishes for England'. While the *Berlin*'s most likely target was the merchant shipping that

THE CREW OF THE *BERLIN* ON BOARD THEIR SHIP. RUDOLF KÄMMERER IS PROBABLY AMONG THEM, ALTHOUGH IT HAS NOT BEEN POSSIBLE TO IDENTIFY HIM FOR CERTAIN.

operated between Liverpool and the United States, the ship's *actual* victim turned out to be far more significant. Little did Rudolf and his comrades know that the mines they laid on the night of 22 October 1914 would strike fear into the heart of the British Admiralty and cause a loss so painful that the British tried to keep it secret.

The *Berlin*, launched in 1908, had started life as a stylish passenger ship plying her trade between New York and the Mediterranean; but with the outbreak of war in August 1914, she was converted to an auxiliary mine-layer. Her first outing a month later, from Germany's North Sea naval base at Wilhelmshaven, was aborted after it was feared that she would be spotted by patrolling British warships. However, on 16 October 1914 she set off again, *en route* to the north coast of Ireland to lay mines. Rudolf, a 25-year-old seaman born in Greussen, near Sondershausen in central Germany, wrote copious notes about the escapade and mockingly attributed its success to 'England's slackness'. After all, the 17,300-ton liner, capable of carrying more than 1,500 passengers, had managed to sneak through British sea barriers and proceeded to sail around the coast of Scotland undetected, before finally reaching the Irish Sea. In his 81-page handwritten account, Rudolf related the lead-up to the mission and ridiculed a British torpedo-boat flotilla he saw guarding the entrance to the North Channel. 'They would never have dreamt that a German ship would dare to come here,' he wrote, adding: 'England, feel free to go back to sleep.' He claimed the intention was to lay the mines on 22 October, to mark the German Empress Augusta's birthday, and in a place where they would 'cause the most damage to England'.

As she approached the North Channel just before dark, the *Berlin* had to pass two British steamers from the White Star Line. 'We motored very slowly and let the steamers go ahead, which mistook us for an English patrol vessel,' Rudolf noted. 'At 10 o'clock in the evening a white light was sighted from Tory Island. Now we had to be doubly careful as we found ourselves right against the Irish coast. A moment later we had to stop, and eased back, because land could be seen in the darkness. Captain-Lieutenant Kirst, who knew the coast like the back of his hand, had immediately noticed that the British had changed their lights. He said to himself: "Old mates you have mixed up the [navigation] lights, but that'll do you no good." Later, on the port side, we saw a flash of light from the Scottish coast too. It was lit a few more times, and at 12 o'clock we found ourselves in the middle of the North Channel. First our intention was to lay the mines near Glasgow, blow up the ship, take to the lifeboats and head to land. The heavy battleships were not far from us. With the active mines we had onboard, one shot from them would be enough to ensure we'd be left with no survivors.' By 12.30am, the *Berlin* started to lay the mines in a zigzag pattern. 'It looked eerily beautiful as the mines plopped into the silver-shining wake,' wrote Rudolf. 'They were placed at anchor, between 4.5 to 5.5 metres below the water surface. By 1.30am the eggs were laid ... We disappeared into the dark night at a speed of about 21 knots.'

The ship, whose top speed under normal conditions was 18.5 knots, laboured and trembled as it was pushed to its limit. By 8.30am she was 138 miles from the British coast and Rudolf noted that Cunard's transatlantic liner *Mauretania* – then Britain's fastest merchant vessel – would be in the area later that morning. Musing about what might happen should she come across the minefield, his notes conclude: 'Now it's war, we can't give aid. We are destined to destroy the enemy.' He boasted that the *Berlin* had already achieved two out of its four tasks: 'The first was to cross the North Sea, and the second – the main task – was to lay the mines,' adding, 'The third is to capture fishing trawlers near Iceland, and finally interrupt the trade around Arkhangel.'

By November, the *Berlin* was stationed off neutral Norway on a mission to intercept ships sailing between Britain and Russia, but after an unsuccessful few weeks, with her coal supplies diminishing and enemy radio traffic increasing, her

A MAP FROM RUDOLF'S DIARY SHOWS THE ROUTE TAKEN BY THE *BERLIN*.

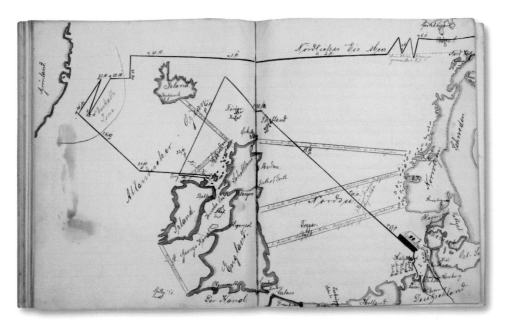

commander decided the ship could not return to Germany and would instead head for Trondheim. However, her arrival at the Norwegian port caused alarm bells to sound; despite taking seven hours to voyage along Trondheim fjord and passing multiple forts on her way, astonishingly no-one had seen her coming. 'The Norwegians call the *Berlin* the ghost ship,' quipped Rudolf. 'The commander of the largest fort received 18 months imprisonment for not seeing us, and his officers received 10 months.'

As an armed vessel in neutral territory, the *Berlin* was immediately classified as a warship and was given 24 hours to leave port; but a lack of fuel and boiler damage meant that she could not meet the deadline, and she was instead interned by the Norwegian authorities. Rudolf recorded that the crew were allowed to keep in touch with their families back home, but they were not permitted to write about their trip. His diary also suggests that they denied any involvement in the previous month's mine-laying operation, with their commander pleading ignorance about large holes in the rear of the vessel – probably created for the release of the mines. The crew only heard about the success of their mission on 25 November 1914 – more than a month after it was completed. 'At 5.30pm, we all had muster at the petty officers' mess, where the first officer told us he went ashore and found out that England's newest and most modern dreadnought *Audacious* and three merchant ships have hit the mines laid by us,' wrote Rudolf. 'The German fleet sent the crew of the auxiliary cruiser *Berlin* a triple "hurrah".'

The reason it took so long for them to hear this news was because Admiral Sir John Jellicoe, commanding Britain's Grand Fleet – the bulk of the Royal Navy protecting Britain's home waters – had tried to keep it secret. The *Audacious*, a 23,400-ton 'super-dreadnought', had been among the Second Battle Squadron of the Grand Fleet, leaving Loch Swilly on a gunnery exercise on 27 October.[2] She struck a mine on her port side at 8.45am, causing the engine room to flood. In fact, the Germans had had a lucky break because, unbeknownst to them, the Grand Fleet had moved to Loch Swilly from its main base at Scapa Flow, which was having its defences against U-boat attacks improved. Believing there was still a chance of turning back, the *Audacious*'s captain, Cecil F. Dampier, set a course for Loch Swilly at the best manageable speed of 9 knots. However, the flooding was spreading, and all but 250 essential crew were evacuated by boats lowered from the White Star liner RMS *Olympic* and the light cruiser HMS *Liverpool*. Both ships attempted to tow the stricken vessel, but the tow lines snapped. By 8.45pm *Audacious* had capsized, and a short while later she sank.

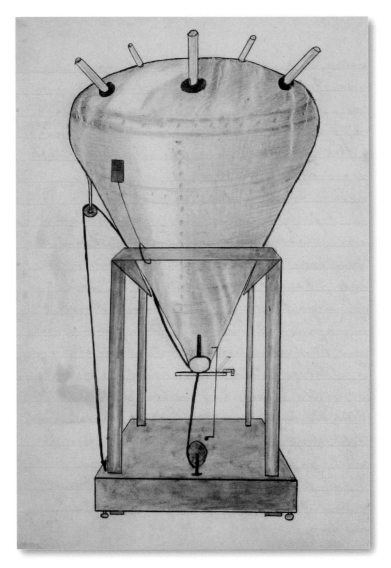

RUDOLF'S DIARY EVEN INCLUDED A DRAWING OF A MINE.

No lives were lost in the incident, but the destruction of Britain's premier battleship was a serious blow to the Admiralty's morale. Jellicoe proposed a blanket ban on any publicity, with the agreement of the Board of Admiralty and the British Cabinet.[3] It meant that *Audacious* continued to appear in fleet lists until after the war – a plan that was open to ridicule as many Americans aboard the *Olympic* had witnessed the incident, and some had even taken photos. Historian Everett Sharpe described the sinking as 'a massive embarrassment' for the Royal Navy, coming so early in the war and, especially, so close to home: 'It showed the Admiralty how vulnerable their much vaunted dreadnought battleships were to German mines,' he said. 'They wanted to cover up the sinking because it was hugely damaging to the reputation of the Royal Navy, which was seen as the senior service. They had lost a super-dreadnought to a mine in home territorial waters when they had been expecting ship-to-ship action in the waters of the North Sea. There is also the possibility that it created a greater worry of failure among senior Royal Navy officers; it definitely damaged the Admiralty's credibility as the British plan to keep it quiet backfired because almost every other nation wrote about and discussed the loss.'

As for the crew of the *Berlin*, they were detained in Norway for the duration of the war, although a few members did attempt to escape. In 1919 the liner was handed over to Britain as part of the defeated Germany's war reparations and sold to the White Star Line in 1920, where she was refitted and renamed *Arabic* in 1921. She initially sailed the Southampton to New York service, before being finally broken up in 1931.

Endnotes

1 Sir Edward Grey was British foreign secretary between 1905 and 1916 – and thus the longest continuously serving British foreign secretary in history. To him was attributed the famous verdict as war broke: 'The lamps are going out all over Europe, we shall not see them lit again in our time.'

2 'Dreadnought' – a type of battleship with heavy-calibre guns and steam turbine propulsion. They were based on the advanced design of HMS *Dreadnought*, unveiled by the Royal Navy in 1906, and a race to build dreadnoughts ensued between Britain and Germany. 'Super-dreadnoughts' were even more powerful.

3 In *A History of the Great War 1914–1918* (1934), C.R.M.F. Cruttwell wrote: 'In view of the desperate military situation in Flanders, and of Turkish neutrality yet hanging precariously in the balance, the Cabinet agreed to keep the loss secret. Although many passengers on the *Olympic* had seen and even photographed the sinking vessel, although the disaster was subject of common gossip, not even a rumour appears to have reached Germany for at least five weeks.'

'Our friends the enemy'
THE CHRISTMAS TRUCE

Just after Signaller Bernard Brookes had finished cleaning his bicycle, following a morning on duty, he and a comrade decided to explore a badly shelled factory. It was a sunny afternoon on Christmas Eve 1914, and apart from scouting around for souvenirs such as shell heads and other war trophies, what intrigued the pair was a large hole near the top of a high chimney that stretched above the building. 'Of course we should not have been near the place, but it was interesting,' admitted Bernard, in the diary he wrote months after the war. [1] 'My chum, who knew something of factories, mentioned that if we got through the furnace we would be able to go inside the chimney – and being a clear day – we might get a view behind the German lines. I suggested that he should lead the way, so he crawled through the grate and I followed.' Using rungs inside the chimney, the pair climbed to the top, but with every step the other man made, Bernard – who referred to the Germans as 'Germs' – got covered in soot and dust. 'We reached the

shell hole, and with a pair of field glasses, saw the Germs a mile or so behind the firing line – some working, others walking or cycling, carts with rations or wounded men passing along the roads in rear of their lines,' he said. Afterwards, the pair returned to Headquarters to find the Germans had turned their fire on the factory. 'Evidently we had been spotted and the Bosches thought that it was an

▶
SERGEANT BERNARD BROOKES,
PICTURED IN JANUARY 1917.
A SMALL GOLD STRIPE ON HIS LEFT CUFF
INDICATES THAT HE HAS BEEN WOUNDED.

observation station, and every now and again they would send a few shells at the factory, so we were instrumental in wasting the Germs' ammunition,' said Bernard. 'At any rate, I hope that we choose for our observation stations cleaner places than this chimney.'

It was the first Christmas of the war, and Bernard had been in the Queen's Westminster Rifles for four months and at the front for just two weeks. Born in 1893, one of six children to notary clerk Samuel Brookes and his wife Martha Ann Brookes (*née* Daniel), Bernard had been on a cycling holiday through Gloucestershire and South Wales in the summer, when news came through of the assassination of Archduke Franz Ferdinand of Austria-Hungary and his wife, in Sarajevo. It was the beginning of the international crisis that led to war. When Britain declared war on 4 August, Bernard was eager to enlist. He had assurances that his job at the Belgian firm Bungee & Co. would be kept open throughout the hostilities and his full salary paid, so he and two colleagues headed to the central London recruiting office of the 16th Battalion of the County of London Regiment, the Queen's Westminster Rifles – a territorial battalion that was part of the 6th Division. After a two-hour wait, he was sworn in, passed as fit and given a free pass to travel on the motor omnibuses in civilian clothes. 'With large ideas of spending the winter in Egypt and on the whole having a rather good holiday (but not with the slightest thought of fighting or danger) we proudly agreed to serve in foreign lands,' he wrote.

To his surprise, Bernard was appointed as a signaller. A keen cyclist, he was offered £5 for his bike by army officials (although he only actually received £3 and 15 shillings), and was later allowed to use it to carry out his signalling work in France. 'Why I was picked out for this duty, I really cannot say ... but I took a liking to signalling, found it very interesting and not at all monotonous,' he said. Unlike his fellow infantrymen, signallers were not expected to be involved in digging, guard duty, or dirty work – and they often had more comfortable digs, such as a dry barn, rather than a cold, wet trench. Their job was to read maps, send messages by Morse code, mend damaged communication lines, and, before they left for France, to help the Post Office send out telegrams and 'tender messages to sweethearts and wives'. Bernard commented in his diary that he hoped all the missives 'arrived at their destinations with the wording correct, but I have my doubts'. However, he was positive about the task ahead and told his mother in a final letter home before leaving England on 1 November 1914: 'I am very glad to have this experience and feel sure of my safety.'

On the evening of 24 December 1914, Bernard and his battalion were staying at a farm near La Chapelle d'Armentières in northern France, very close to the front line. 'Towards the evening the Germs became very hilarious, singing and shouting out to us,' he recorded. 'They said in English that if we did not fire, they would not, and eventually it was arranged that shots should not be exchanged. With this they lit fires outside their trench, and sat round and commenced a concert; incidentally singing some English songs to the accompaniment of a bugle band. A Germ officer carrying a lantern came slightly forward and asked to see one of our officers to arrange a truce for tomorrow (Xmas Day). An officer went out (after we had stood at our posts with rifles loaded in case of treachery) and arrangements were made that between 10am and noon, and from 2pm to 4pm tomorrow, intercourse between the Germs and ourselves should take place. It was a beautiful night and a sharp frost set in, and when we awoke in the morning the ground was covered with a white raiment. It was indeed an ideal Christmas, and the spirit of peace and goodwill was very striking in comparison with the hatred and death-dealing of the past few months. One appreciated in a new light the meaning of Christianity, for it certainly was marvellous that such a change in the attitude of the opposing armies could be wrought by an event which happened nigh on 2,000 years ago.'

Bernard's Christmas Day began with an early morning mission to find two men who had disappeared overnight. After checking the dressing station in Chapelle d'Armentières a mile away, word came from the Germans that the pair had walked into their trench 'in a state which proved that they had "drunk of the loving cup, not wisely, but too well"'. They were interned in a civilian camp, and by 9am Bernard, a practising Catholic, was given permission to go to Mass at a nearby church which he had come across while looking for the missing men. 'This church was terribly shelled, and was within the range of rifle fire, as was clearly proved by the condition of the wall facing the trenches, and no effort had been made to clear the wreckage, as to attempt this would have been fraught with danger,' he wrote. 'A priest, however, had come in from Armentières to minister to the few people who were still living in the district. In this church which would hold about 300, there were some 30 people, and I was the only soldier. It was indeed a unique service, and during a short address which the priest gave, I was about the only one who was not crying, and that was because I did not understand much of what was being said.'

Bernard returned to his duties between noon and 2pm, where he enjoyed Bully beef, potatoes, Christmas pudding and red wine, which had been found in one of the cellars on the farm. 'In the afternoon I went out and had a chat with "our friends the enemy",' he remembered. 'Many of the Germs had costumes on which had been taken from the houses nearby, and one facetious fellow had a blouse, skirt, top hat and umbrella, which grotesque figure caused much merriment. Various souvenirs were exchanged which I managed to send home. We also had an opportunity of seeing the famous Iron Cross which some of the men wore attached to a black and white riband. These crosses are very well made and have an edging of silver. The man's name is engraved on one side, and the reason of the award briefly stated on the other. I have also a number of Germ signatures and addresses on a fly leaf of my "Active Service Pay Book" and it was arranged that at the end of the war we would write one to the other if we came through safely. [2] The Germs wanted to continue a partial truce until the New Year, for as some of them said, they were heartily sick of the war and did not want to fight, but as we were leaving the trenches early next morning and naturally did not want them to know, we insisted on the truce ending at midnight, at which time our artillery sent over to them four shells of small calibre to let them know that the truce, at which the whole world would wonder, was ended and in its place, death and bloodshed would once again reign supreme.'

By the end of May 1915, Bernard and his battalion had moved into Belgium, and in August that year the Queen's Westminster Rifles were operating in the Hooge sector, near Ypres, where the Germans launched their first flamethrower attack against the British. On 9 August 1915, Bernard had already been 'over the top' twice at Sanctuary Wood with messages to captured trenches, because all communication wires had been

▶

THE SANCTUARY WOOD TRENCH SYSTEM (AS IT APPEARS TODAY), WHERE BERNARD SUFFERED SHELLSHOCK.
© STEPHEN BULL.

broken. 'About noon a message was received from Headquarters that the trenches were to be held "at all costs", and this order had to be delivered in the captured lines,' said Bernard. 'It was given to one Signaller but he never returned. Again the message was sent up an hour or so later, and again the Signaller failed to reach his objective. The bombardment was still going on fiercely, when at about 3pm, our Major came to me and said that as I knew the way, and had been across twice successfully, he wished me to make another trip and get the message through. I started out "over the top" and a machine gun opened up, and I had no other option but to drop into a communication trench nearby which was filled with water and dead men. In this communication trench lay the men of the K.R.Rs [King's Royal Rifle Corps] who had been caught up by the liquid fire a few days previously, and the three letters which they wear on the epaulets on the shoulder, will always be engraved on my mind.'

As a 17-inch German gun continued to fire, Bernard made his way along the communication trench. 'I was soaked to the skin and covered in mud, and I found it was impossible to continue along this trench. I therefore jumped out on top, and with my rifle smothered in mud and bayonet fixed, got within 10 to 12 yards of the captured trench. It was then that a salvo of shells burst just above my head and threw me very heavily to the ground but I was not hit. Some men in our trench spotted me and ran out to give me a hand into the trench. As far as I remember, there were about half a dozen men left who were not wounded and no officers at all. I gave them the written message, and as I had to get back and report that I had delivered my message, two men who had been wounded decided to come with me, and as I was unable to walk by myself, gave me a hand back to my station. They took me to the Major and said that I had delivered my message, and we were all talking when another shell burst nearby; throwing a mass of dirt, wood, etc., all over us. I was then taken out of the trenches, and cannot say that I remember much more until travelling in an ambulance to hospital in Vlamertinghe.'

Bernard was placed on a stretcher next to wounded German prisoners at a field hospital. 'Later on I was wakened, and the orderly proceeded to arouse the Germs, and their nerves were so affected, that they both jumped up and commenced fighting. This so completely upset me, that it put the finishing touch, and I was from that time in a state of semi-consciousness and could not speak. I then remember being put in the hospital train in my damp and wet clothes, waking up during the day of Tuesday the 10th August in a nice comfortable bed in a hospital at Camiers near Etaples. Thus I made my exit from Belgium into France.'

Bernard had suffered shellshock and was returned to England aboard the hospital ship HS *Brighton* on 12 August 1915. After several weeks at Saint Anselm's VAD (Voluntary Aid Detachment) Hospital, Walmer, near Deal in Kent, he was hospitalised again in Chelsea, before being sent to a military hospital at Epsom for convalescence. He never returned to the front line, and after his discharge as a patient at Epsom was taken onto the military staff. He rose gradually from the rank of lance corporal to sergeant in charge of an orderly room at the hospital, which contained over 4,500 troops from Britain and its colonies. He also introduced and edited a magazine to cheer up the patients – *The Monthly Tonic*. After the war, Bernard met and married teacher Nora Una Cole at St Anselm's Catholic Church in Tooting Bec, London, on 15 May 1919 and they settled in Sanderstead, Surrey. Bernard started work at the French bank Société Générale de Paris, and the couple went on to have five children. He died in 1962, several months after suffering a stroke.

Bernard's daughter Una Barrie said her father's diary had provided the family with a fascinating insight into life on the front line. 'Dad was only in the war a year, but he kept notes at the time, which was probably against regulations. He didn't think he was anyone special – he just wanted to record what it had been like to be a soldier in the war. He didn't just recall the battles, but also the extraordinary things that happened to him. The war helped him develop a taste for smoking a pipe and drinking rum, which he claimed was the only thing that had kept the troops alive when they were knee-deep in mud and water. But while he never regretted joining up and attended many Queen's Westminster reunions, the shellshock he suffered had a lasting effect through his life. He was extremely nervous and jittery and absolutely hated loud noises. The last straw was when I tried to teach myself the violin as a child. He couldn't bear the sound and I had to give it up. He just liked peace and quiet.'

Endnotes

1 His notes were later turned by his daughter Una Barrie into the book *A Signaller's War*, sold in aid of the Royal British Legion.
2 Bernard framed the German signatures he collected on Christmas Day 1914 and hung them on the stairs at the family home in Sanderstead, Surrey. However, after he and Nora retired, the couple moved to Warlingham in the early 1960s and the signatures disappeared. They later emerged at a Bonhams auction in March 2009, where they were sold by an unknown vendor for £1,080.

'Injustice and fate'
A TALE OF CASUAL REVENGE?

IVER AND WIEBKE JUHLER
(*RIGHT*), WITH JOHANN
AND BOTILLE STAMP.

Iver Simonsen Juhler and Wiebke Stamp had been married almost three years and were expecting their first child when Iver received his papers to go to war on 2 August 1914. The couple had just settled in Arnum, in Southern Jutland – a disputed region also known as North Schleswig, and the subject of a war between Denmark and Prussia in the 1860s. But from that time until 1920, the region was part of Germany, and it was here that Iver ran a farm and managed a wooden wheel-making workshop. With war breaking out, it was with a heavy heart that he left his pregnant wife to join a *Landwehr* Infantry Regiment. According to his family he had no desire for warfare or to fight for the German cause; yet within months he was ordered to the Eastern Front against Russia. He was sent to Biala, in Austrian Galicia, but then he contracted typhoid. [1]

Iver was transferred home to recover, giving him the long awaited opportunity to meet his little daughter Elsine, who was born on 6 February 1915. But he had only been home a few weeks when, according to his family, he was told to report to a field hospital in Toftlund. There he was declared healthy and ordered to return to the front. To his family, this was an unusual turn of events, because not only had he done one tour of duty, but he had a farm, he was newly married, and he had a baby daughter; and he had almost certainly not recovered from his illness. It is possible there may not have been anything very unusual about his being returned to war at that time. His field notebook reveals that after falling ill with typhoid, he returned to his company, had a short time on leave, and then spent a month in Toftlund with diphtheria. He was rested for two weeks before returning to his company in Neubrandenburg, and it was a few months later that he reported back to the front. Nevertheless, his family believes there was a sinister reason behind the decision.

Years earlier, his widowed mother-in-law Kathrine Johanne Stamp – who lived in Ullerup, 9 miles south of Arnum – had sent Wiebke's sister Karen to a high school in

Denmark. At the time, Southern Jutland was a society divided between its 'German-minded' and 'Danish-minded' inhabitants – a residual legacy even today. But during the First World War, these were still potent divisions, with families determined to retain the identities of their birth. It was against this background that Kathrine's decision not to send her daughter to a German school brought her into conflict with those favouring a Germanisation of North Schleswig. [2] The group, whose mission was to force the spread of the German language, its people and culture, was led locally by regional Mayor Lindemann from Toftlund and the German Reverend Jacobsen of Skaerbaek. They tried to scupper Kathrine's plans, believing that the Hejls Ungdomsskole (Hejls Youth School) where her daughter Karen attended did not act 'in the German national spirit'. Kathrine was threatened that if she did not remove Karen from the school, she would be sentenced to a fine of 100 marks. When Kathrine refused to change her mind, she was indeed fined and given two weeks to comply or face the threat of a further 150-mark penalty. Her appeal was dismissed by a court in Flensburg, which claimed that she was exposing her daughter to the hazard of 'Danisation' and that she was acting against her late husband's will and wishes, because it was claimed that he 'was of a determined German mind and an opponent of the Danish efforts'. If Karen stayed at the Hejls School it would be 'against both state interests, her father's intentions and especially for the obvious detriment of the child itself'. The court continued: 'The inoculation of anti-German spirit muddies a memory full of piety of the German-minded, deceased father and moreover makes the daughter unhappy and hostile against the state, which is her home, of which she is a citizen, and in which she most likely will have to live.' However, Kathrine Stamp appealed to the Chamber Court in Berlin, and in December 1897 the judgment was set aside and the fines dropped. Karen was allowed to remain in the Danish high school, leaving the mayor and the churchman to read about their humiliating defeat in the newspapers. [3]

According to Iver's grandson, Iver Fromsejer, it was Mayor Lindemann who later recognised Iver Juhler as Kathrine's son-in-law while he was recovering from typhoid – and it was the mayor who ordered him to the field hospital in Toftlund and had him sent back to the front. Was this the case? On the one hand, it would have been quite unusual for a mayor to have the power to send a local man back to an army hospital, as jurisdiction over these kinds of questions lay with the *Stellvertretende Generalkommando*, the military institution that had taken over most local responsibilities from civil authorities after the outbreak of war. On the other hand, the local mayor and churchman were not politicians but civil servants, and they might have been seen as working as local agents with local knowledge of interest for the military command; it is also possible that the German military authorities had simply been following standard policy and procedure. [4]

Whatever the case, Iver was later transferred from the Eastern to the Western Front in France, where he served in the Grand Duke of Mecklenburg's Grenadier-Regiment No. 89, part of the 17th Division that was engaged in attempting to resist the Allies' final push to victory – their Hundred Days Offensive. In a heartfelt and deeply religious letter written to his wife, his father and his daughter on 16 September 1918, Iver expressed his longing to come home, adding poignantly: 'If it is destined for me to stay here, then I pray our dear God that we may gather by the dear God the Father in heaven. And this I beg you my dear wife and father, be good-natured towards one another and make it as easy as possible for yourselves and take good care of the little girl's upbringing and do not forget her. But my dear ones, it is my fervent prayer to God that I may come home and once again live with all of you, my dear ones.' Sadly, Iver died two days after writing that letter in Aizy–Jouy, on the ridge of the much fought over Chemin des Dames in northern France. According to the regimental history, Iver's company and the battalion's 3rd Company repelled a French attack on

A POSTCARD FROM IVER TO WIEBKE, MARKED 'GRENADIER-REGIMENT NO. 89' AND DATED 23 JUNE 1918.

18 September, and their 100 men took 150 French prisoners as they tried to hold the Chemin des Dames at all costs.[5] But Iver was one of three soldiers from his company killed in action; another eight were reported missing and two were wounded.

Iver's grandson, Iver Fromsejer, said: 'I feel so badly about the injustice and fate that struck my grandfather, especially as it changed our lives forever. My mother [Elsine] was only three-years-old when her father was killed. Iver's father, Peter Jessen Juhler, had to help Wiebke run the farm, and his death was yet another blow to Kathrine Stamp, who had already lost her son Johan Stamp in the war. I grew up with Wiebke when she lived with my parents; she was in charge of running the house while my mum and dad ran a nursery garden in Skaerbaek. In quiet times she told me that Iver had been the love of her life, which was why she never married again. He had dearly wanted to be a father and longed to watch his daughter grow up. Sadly, the war – and I believe, revenge – snatched those dreams away.'

Endnotes

1 Since 1951 Biala has been part of Bielsko-Biala, Poland, having been joined with the neighbouring city of Bielsko.

2 *The Sønderjyske Aarbøger* [Yearbooks of South Jutland], 1991, pp. 116–17, note the 'School Association' of South Jutlanders who supported Danish schools over the border, which prompted Germany's *Hamburger Nachrichten* newspaper to opine in 1896: 'Seen from the German-national position this anti-German school "association" carries an immense danger in itself ... As children grow older, their Danishness will intensify ... And as the number of children indoctrinated rises, the numbers of young, protesting men increases significantly.'

3 Peder Meyhoff's book *Meyhoff-slægten* [The Meyhoff Family], 2007, p.55, cites Kathrine's story as representative of a wider culture of repression: 'Between 1897 and 1901, Ernst M. von Köller – the so-called upper President of Prussia – conducted an unusually tough policy of repression against the Danish movement in North Schleswig. Many Danish-born servants and optants – i.e. people from Schleswig, who

had chosen to define themselves as Danish – were expelled, while other families were threatened with losing custody of their younger children, because like Kathrine ... they had sent their children to schools in Denmark.'

4 In a case with parallels to that of Iver, Danishman Peter Hansen Holm (1880–1977) also claimed he was returned to the front as a result of rumours that he was 'Danish-minded'. He recorded in his memoirs how he had taken part in the fighting at Verdun (1916), the Argonne Woods (1916) and on the Somme (1916 to 1917), and that 'in between battles, I was ordered back as quartermaster at the battalion in Flensburg. But one day our County Mayor had reported that they had me under suspicion of being Danish-minded and the result thereof was that I received a letter from The Army Command stating that I immediately had to return back to the front, where I soon after – January 15th 1917 – was wounded in the leg'.

5 Ernst Zipfer, *Geschichte des Grossherzoglich Mecklenburgischen Grenadier-Regiments Nr 89*, 1932.

'It was me who killed him'
HAUNTED BY AN ACT OF WAR

It was a nickname that lasted a lifetime. John Ernest Trousdell Drever – known as 'Old Trousdell' to his mates – was given the unusual middle name after the doctor who delivered him on 14 May 1879. The fifth of nine children, John was born just hours after his twin sister Jemima, to Jemima Drever (*née* Rendall) and George Drever, an agricultural labourer, at the family croft of North Tuan on Westray – one of about 70 islands that make up Scotland's Orkney archipelago.

By 1907, John had met and married Jane Miller, and the couple lived with Jane's parents at Taftend on Westray, where her father, William, was a crofter and kelp-maker – a hard, physical job, which involved collecting seaweed from the shore, drying it and burning it in pits to create kelp ash, which was used in the manufacture of glass and soap. While John worked on the croft, caring for the horses, he subsidised his income by carting goods – including animal feed, groceries and ironmongery – to the local shop from a cargo steamship that shuttled among the islands. Jane also helped the family collect kelp, even when she was expecting their first child in 1912. 'One day as John left to take the cart to the pier, he told her not to go and work in the kelp as it was unsafe in her condition,' said John's great-nephew Tom Muir. 'But after he had gone, her father made her go and gather the heavy, wet kelp and carry it up the beach. The strain caused her to go into labour and she miscarried the baby, a little boy they named George, raising a stone to him in the graveyard at Pierowall, Westray. They never had any children after that.'

After war broke out in August 1914, many Orcadians joined the Seaforth Highlanders, a regiment that recruited from the Scottish Highlands. However, some joined other regiments, such as the Argylls, or the Black Watch (Royal Highland Regiment) and Gordons. It is thought that John joined the Seaforths briefly before serving with the Black Watch and finally the Labour Corps: certainly, his medal card shows him as a private in these last two, and it confirms that he was awarded the Victory and British War medals. The Black Watch got its name from the dark tartan they wore in their kilts, and from their original army role to 'watch' the Highlands. Tom Muir said his family understood that as a private in the Black Watch, John had served on the Western Front and it was there that he was involved in hand-to-hand

JOHN DREVER IN HIGHLAND UNIFORM,
WITH HIS WIFE JANE.

JOHN'S BROTHER ROBERT DREVER IN THE UNIFORM
OF THE 'BIG RED ONE' AMERICAN 1ST DIVISION, WHICH WAS THE FIRST
U.S. FORMATION TO LAND IN FRANCE DURING THE WAR.

combat with the enemy. [1] 'My mother told me that when he was fighting in France, he and his comrades had gone into a village, when one of them shouted a warning to him,' said Tom. 'He swung around just in time to see a German soldier standing behind him. He didn't have time to stop and think – he reacted instinctively like he had been trained – and he thrust a bayonet into the German soldier's stomach and killed him. That act of self-preservation did not make him a hero in his own eyes, but haunted him for the rest of his life. He returned to Westray after the war and tossed his medals into a chest, closing the lid on them. When he was asked why he wouldn't wear them, or attend the Armistice Day Parade, he would reply sadly: "There's a mother in Germany crying for her son – and it was me who killed him. That's nothing to feel proud about."'

By the time the war was over, two of John's younger brothers, David and Robbie, had already emigrated to the United States, while another brother, George, had settled in Westray with his wife Davina. John ran his own small subsistence farm, raising cattle and growing crops on the island to feed them. When his wife died in 1957, John went to live with his niece Jemima, who was known affectionately as 'Mimo'. It was during this time that the family discovered how badly John's wartime experience had affected him. 'It was at night that he suffered the most, crying out in his sleep; reliving that awful moment when he had to kill another man face-to-face,' said Tom. 'One night Mimo was woken up by a thumping noise coming from Uncle Johnny's room. When she went in and switched on the light, she saw him on his knees in the bed throttling the pillow and banging it against the end of the bed. The light woke him up and he collapsed on the bed, saying: "That old German will just not die." He never forgave himself for what he had done and had nightmares for the rest of his life.'

Tom said that he regularly visited his Great-uncle John as a child, although he described the trip by boat from his home in Kirkwall to Westray as a tortuous one, involving many hours at sea. 'To me he was just a lovely, old guy. He was quite quiet, but cheery, and when he couldn't light his pipe, I'd do it for him. The family openly talked about him having killed this German soldier, which I found hard to reconcile with the gentle character that I knew. It was obviously something he could not come to terms with either, but there was no counselling or therapy available then to help him broken bodies were accepted after the First World War, but not broken minds. My mother always gave the impression that while she thought it was a terrible incident, she was quite proud of him.'

John died in Mosside, Westray, in 1975, just short of his 96th birthday, and is buried in the quiet graveyard at Pierowall by the sea, alongside his wife and their lost baby.

Endnotes

1 During the First World War, the Black Watch fought mainly in France and Flanders, except for the 2nd Battalion, which also fought on the Mesopotamian and Palestine fronts, and the 10th and 13th battalions, which also saw service in the Balkans. The 2nd Battalion was even briefly merged with 1st Battalion, Seaforth Higlanders, early in 1916 to form a 'Highland Battalion' within one of the Indian brigades. Further information on the battalions and regiments can be found in E.A. James, *British Regiments 1914–1918*, New Edition, London, 1978, pp. 83–5 and 103–4.

'Just a piece of shrapnel'
THE MAN FROM THE PRU'S BIG ADVENTURE

Eight months after he was called up to join the British Army, junior office clerk Alan Ray found himself fighting in the heart of the Second Battle of Ypres – the 1915 German offensive that witnessed poison gas on the Western Front for the first time, and where the Allies' hold on their salient around Ypres shrank. Charles William Alan Ray, known as Alan, was born on 29 December 1893. He was therefore in his 20th year, and living with his father Charles, a tobacco merchant, and mother Lily, in Brixton, South London, when war broke out. As a Territorial – one of the army's 'part-timers' – Alan received his joining papers for the 5th City of London Battalion (London Rifle Brigade), The London Regiment, on 5 August 1914.[1] By September, Alan had swapped a cosy office at the Prudential insurance company in Holborn, London, for a freezing training camp on top of Crowborough Beacon in Sussex, which he described as being 'as bleak a camp as is possible to

TELEGRAM DATED 4 AUGUST 1914, ORDERING ALAN RAY TO MOBILISE.

imagine. All the medical officers have condemned it and even when the sun shines it is bitterly cold.' In his regular missives to his mother, which illustrate exactly what life was like for a young private away from family for a lengthy period of time, Alan shared his experiences and requested that many home comforts be sent, including parcels of food, clothing, tobacco, sweets and alcohol.

Alan's adventures began in November 1914, when the battalion left Southampton for France. After the ferry crossing and a lengthy train journey, Alan told his mother in a letter dated 12 November: 'We are quartered at a monastery and are being put through strenuous training ... The weather is not the kind usually associated with sunny France and it has caused four of our horses to peg out.' By December, he was on front-line service, assuring her: 'Everything is quite alright out here and our total losses to date are four men killed and about 20 wounded. Harry Lidbury is safe and sound and has had quite a lot of exciting times. He has been out sniping at night and has crawled on his stomach to within four or five yards of the advance German trenches. Jimmy Cole has found a soft job and is a clerk at the Brigade headquarters where he ought not to come to much harm. As no doubt you have seen in the papers, the King is out here reviewing the troops and today he was passing very close by us and we sent a couple of companies for the parade. Of course we are wishing we were going to be at home for Xmas but I think we shall have quite a good time so long as we are well backed up with eatables from home, as it is next to impossible to buy anything here as the Germans have ransacked the place when they were here a month ago. I only wish you had sent the socks with the last parcels as I am on my last pair now and washing is out of the question. I don't know if you are aware that we do not carry kitbags with us, so I think you will agree it is time I had a change of clothing. Two pairs of Aertex drawers and a flannel shirt with the socks would make a lot of difference to my comfort. Would you ask the Govnor [sic] to send me out two briar pipes, one a bulldog with an ordinary straight stem for a pal of mine, and a light stemmed one for me. [2] Ask him to pick out two nice ones as we have time to appreciate a good smoke. Two or three pounds of Mackintoshes Toffee and some chocolate and almonds and raisins will help keep us alive; please put in as much as you can. There are plenty of "souvenirs", as the French people call them, in the shape of German helmets and pieces of shells, but I am not troubling to collect any because I think there is plenty of time yet before we shall have a chance of bringing them back to England.'

By 11 December 1914, Alan was reporting that while everything was going 'quite smoothly ... the casualty list is gradually getting bigger and I suppose by now we have about a dozen killed and close on 40 wounded.' But while Christmas Day began fairly quietly, Alan reported an unexpected turn of events in the trenches. 'We have had a weird, though quite enjoyable time, and passed our day just like any other in the week. We started off by watering and feeding the horses, had our breakfast at 8 o'clock; we then spent the morning cleaning our horses and retired for dinner at 1.30pm. [3] We dined off roast beef, harvest beans and potatoes, with Xmas pudding and rum to follow – so you see that we did not do so badly. Unfortunately, I had to turn out with my van directly afterwards to take grub and presents to the men in the trenches and we did not get back 'til 7.30. Nevertheless, I thought of everyone at home at 3 o'clock when I was jolting along over the cobble stones. I think Xmas in the trenches must have been even more weird. The Germans came out of their trenches together with our own men and they made two big fires and everybody sang carols and songs, while the officers drank together. The men gave each other souvenirs and some of our men have got addresses of Germans for them to write to after the war.'

It was with great excitement that Alan reported on 17 February 1915 that he had had his first bath in France, adding that the experience – along with 'fresh clean under-clothing' – had left him 'elated'. Two months later, a letter from Easter 1915 reveals that the Allies were not so keen to repeat the Christmas truce. 'I can't remember if I told you in my last letter about the Germans asking for a truce on Good Friday? They wanted to repeat the Xmas program, but our fellows would have none of it and gave them five rounds rapid to think about,' his letter of 14 April 1915 states. 'The Germans then put over some rifle grenades and wounded one or two of our chaps.' Less than two weeks later, Alan found himself joining the ranks of the wounded, and in a very understated way informed his 'dear mother' from Northampton General Hospital on 30 April 'that I have at last managed to stop something. It is nothing terrible, just a piece of shrapnel shell about the width of your thumb nail and about half as wide in the side of my knee, or at least it is not in my knee now as they took it out yesterday.'

Alan received his wound on either 25 or 26 April, days into what would become known as the Second Battle of Ypres. The offensive began on 22 April with the Germans shocking Allied soldiers by bombarding the enemy line with artillery – and then releasing lethal chlorine gas. The gas wafted across no-man's land and into the trenches towards French and Algerian colonial troops, to devastating effect. Chlorine – heavier than air – sank into the trenches, blinding the troops, burning their lungs and, in fatal cases, causing asphyxiation. On 24 April, the Germans launched another gas attack, but this time the breeze carried it into Canadian positions just west of the village of St Julien, four miles north of Ypres. The Canadians improvised gas masks, by urinating on their handkerchiefs and placing them over their noses and mouths to protect their airways; however, this was generally ineffective and the German troops took the village, leaving over 3,000 Canadian casualties.

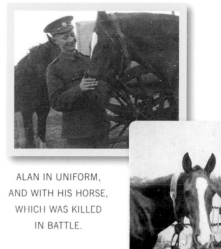

ALAN IN UNIFORM, AND WITH HIS HORSE, WHICH WAS KILLED IN BATTLE.

It was therefore just after this onslaught that Alan was injured. In his letter from hospital he wrote that his battalion had left 'Plug Street' – the village of Ploegsteert – for a three-week rest at Steenwerck, about six or seven miles behind the firing line; but after six days they were ordered to move on.[4] 'We took the Transport to Bailleul and entrained there at midday for Poperinghe where we stopped the night. Next morning at five we left for Vlamertinghe where we could hear the shells in the distance whistling. We had time there to have some grub and to groom our horses and wash ourselves. Vlamertinghe is just a small town three or four miles behind Ypres and last Sunday when we got there it was packed with wounded mostly Canadians who have lost very heavily. They had been in the trenches for the two days previous without food or water as transports could get nowhere near for the shells and it was our duty to go and relieve them, which we started today at 5.30 on Sunday evening. We could tell it was pretty hot further up as the wounded were coming down in a continual stream. Those who weren't hit in the legs were walking; some were riding in empty RA limbers and the serious cases were going in the Red Cross motors.[5] When we got near Ypres we were given the order to gallop as the place was being bombarded and you can guess we had an exciting ride for a couple of miles. Of course the place is very much torn about and dead horses and broken carts were fairly numerous on the roadside. At least we got to a little village called St Jean on top of a hill. We called a halt just outside a dressing station where there were four or five motor ambulances and it was here that shrapnel landed right in the middle of us. It laid out quite a few of us and I won't tell you what it looked like afterwards as it is not very pleasant. At any rate, after much travelling in boats, trains, motors,

A POSTCARD SHOWS ALAN (*FOURTH FROM LEFT, SEATED*)
WITH OTHERS FROM THE 'LRB' – LONDON RIFLE BRIGADE.

etc., I have arrived in Northampton, and am feeling quite alright in myself although of course my leg is not yet usable. There is no need at all for you to panic and I hope it will not be long before I get the chance of coming to see you all. In the meantime there are one or two things I want you to send me as I lost everything I had when my horses ran away with my limber and I didn't feel like running after them.'

Alan kept a photo of his beloved horse, which was killed during the battle. On the back of it, his son John Betson Ray wrote: 'Pa horse killed under him. Pa's knee (left) injured suffered limp.' It is unclear whether Alan returned to active service in Belgium after he was wounded, although his family still possess an artillery shell from a few weeks later, engraved 'Ypres – June 1915', which they used as a dinner bell. However, at some point he was promoted acting corporal and posted to 2/17th County of London Battalion, Poplar and Stepney Rifles. The next that is heard from him is in May 1917, when he sent a letter home during active service in Salonika.[6] In it, he wrote far less about casualties and hardship, and more about entertainment and seeing the sights. However, in a letter dated 21 August 1918, he wrote to say that he had been in Egypt to join his unit but had to be evacuated to hospital in Italy having suffered pneumonia.

Alan returned to civilian life at the Prudential after the war, where he met and married Mary Scott from the typing pool, and the couple had two children: John Betson and Patricia. Alan had a successful career at the 'Pru', working his way up to become director – a position he also held on the boards of Technicolor and Rugby Cement, among other companies. According to his family he had a limp and used to complain about the after-effects of the gas attack at Ypres – though he was also a lifelong pipe smoker. He died in 1972, aged 78.

Alan's grandson Simon Ray has since located the exact spot where Alan was injured, by the dressing station at St Jean, a sleepy suburb of Ypres: 'The corner where the field station stood is now a nondescript bar with moustachioed locals drinking beer on a Saturday morning,' he said, adding: 'It's a strange feeling looking down the road from where he came. Alan was 20 when the First World War started, and I look back at how I saw the world when I was his age. Clichéd, but life was one big adventure, and mortality was not even on the horizon, so for Alan and his comrades to be confronted by such carnage at such a young age really focuses the mind. They must have grown up pretty quickly.'

Endnotes

1 The 5th City of London Battalion, London Rifle Brigade, was part of the all-Territorial London Regiment, the largest infantry regiment in the British Army. It had many different cap badges for its battalions. That of the 5th was the Royal Arms surrounded by an oak wreath and topped with a crown. Many of the London battalions drew on local men or those united by their profession.

2 'Govnor' – a reference to Alan's father who, being a tobacco merchant, was in a position to supply pipes and cigarettes.

3 The horses Alan mentions are likely to have been ones that pulled wagons with the battalion's equipment and baggage.

4 Ploegsteert or 'Plug Street' was to the south of Ypres, very close to the French border. The Ploegsteert Memorial commemorates more than 11,000 British and South African 'missing' servicemen, who died in the area during the First World War but have no known grave.

5 'RA Limbers' – Royal Artillery limbers, a limber being the piece of equipment resembling a small wheeled cart, usually used for towing a gun, but evidently sometimes also employed to carry the wounded.

6 'Salonika' – the Greek city now known as Thessaloniki. The Salonika Front, or Macedonian Front, was opened in northern Greece by the Allies in 1915. It began as an attempt to (unsuccessfully) prevent Serbia being overrun by Austria-Hungary, Germany and Bulgaria. For much of its time, the front and its encampments were criticised for their relative inactivity in prosecuting the war.

'Soul mates'
CAPTIVE HEARTS IN THE TRENTINO

It was not the most romantic location for a couple to meet and fall in love. Katzenau was a notorious internment camp, built on the banks of the River Danube to hold thousands of Austro-Hungarian citizens suspected of being pro-Italian or otherwise politically unreliable. Here, in prison-like conditions, surrounded by barbed-wire fences guarded by sentries carrying bayonets, the inmates lived in wooden huts, which provided little protection against the icy winds that swept the plain in winter or the sweltering summer sun. Among them were 1,700 residents of the Trentino, a mountainous province now part of northern Italy, but which in 1914 was still within the Austro-Hungarian Empire. They were evacuated from their homes, along with 100,000 others along the border, in May 1915, when Italy entered the war against Austria-Hungary and a front opened up through the region.

KATZENAU INTERNMENT CAMP, WHERE EMILIO ALBERINI AND ELSA MASCHLER
WERE SENT BY THE AUSTRO-HUNGARIAN AUTHORITIES.

More than 30,000 of them were sent south by the Italian army, while 70,000 were sent north to the central provinces of the Empire. However, some 1,700, whom the authorities suspected of pro-Italian irredentism – a belief that the territory should be returned to Italy – were locked up, often with their families, at Katzenau, more than 300 miles away from home.

Emilio Alberini, a 26-year-old shopkeeper from Borgo Valsugana, a riverside town east of Trento, was one such believer. He was taken with local priest Don Cesare Refatti, a keen photographer and mountaineer: the Austrians believed he might otherwise use his great knowledge of the mountain trails to become a spy for the Italians. The majority of the camp's inmates, though, were elderly people, women, or children, while the men incarcerated with them either were considered unsuitable for military service, either because they could not be trusted, or because of health or other reasons. Emilio had already been rejected because he was considered too short and thin.

Life in the camp was hard, with poor water supplies leading to repeated epidemics of typhus among prisoners. In the first few weeks of internment, there were insufficient quantities of food, bedding and clothing. Inmates were forced to sleep on planks covered with a thin layer of straw, and they had to give up any serious hope of maintaining personal hygiene. But as time went on, the camp expanded – to include a hospital, a church, a prison, sinks, and wooden pavements that linked various buildings across the field to save inmates trudging through the mud. The camp also opened a small shop, from which prisoners could buy foodstuffs such as bread.

It was because of his background in retail that Emilio found himself working in the shop. One of his customers was Elsa Mascher, a willowy dark-haired teenager, who had been evacuated from Arco on the northern shore of Lake Garda with her grandfather, mother and three sisters. The youngster would regularly visit the shop to buy meals for her family and to break the tedium of the daily routine, which involved cleaning the sheds, cooking and washing clothes. In the view of Fulvio Alberini, Emilio's grandson, 'Elsa really caught my grandfather's eye – he thought she was beautiful. Not only did she stand out because she was very tall – taller than him – she had dark brown hair and would always spend time chatting to him. It wasn't long before he fell in love and longed for her to visit again. When she did come, Emilio would give Elsa extra food and some chocolate as a token of his affection. Elsa's sisters soon realised she was getting preferential treatment, so when they needed extra supplies, they would always send her, in the hope she would get something

EMILIO (*FAR RIGHT, STANDING*) AT BENESCHAU, NEAR PRAGUE,
WITH OTHER MEN ENLISTED INTO THE AUSTRO-HUNGARIAN ARMY, *c*.1917.

more. Although Elsa was flattered by the attention and the sweet gifts, in the end she had to tell him: "I don't want chocolate, what I really crave is bread.'"

The couple's love blossomed, and camp life also improved with the introduction of foreign-language courses, talks and music concerts organised to entertain the inmates. However, by spring 1917 Katzenau could not contain all the political internees of Trentino, so numerous groups were sent across Austria, while others were simply moved to other prisons. The decision to disperse them meant that Emilio and Elsa would be parted for the rest of the war. Emilio was sent to Beneschau, near Prague, finally to join the Austro-Hungarian army, where he was ordered to serve well behind the lines. 'By this time they were so short of people, they were even recruiting those they suspected of harbouring pro-Italian feelings,' said Fulvio. 'But because he was not trusted he was never sent to the front line and was tasked with handling supplies instead.' Elsa and her family, meanwhile, were sent to Innsbruck, where they stayed until 1919. As a parting message to the girl he loved, Emilio told Elsa in a letter: 'To my dear, remember me always everywhere, Emilio. I love you and will always think about you. Katzenau, April 1917.'

On 3 November 1918, Italian troops entered Trento. On this date too, Italy and Austria-Hungary agreed an armistice: their war was over, and Trentino was annexed to the victorious Kingdom of Italy. 'After the war Emilio and Elsa returned to their home towns where they found their houses had been completely destroyed,' confirmed Fulvio. 'But Emilio was desperate to see Elsa again and searched Arco until he found her. The couple were reunited and married in 1920. Their daughter Maria was born later that year, and in 1929, they had a son, Emilio, who went on to become my father.'

The family ran a grocery store from the ground floor of their home in Borgo Valsugana until Emilio senior suffered a stroke in the 1950s. Elsa nursed him for more than eight years until his death in 1961, and she continued to live with the family until she died in 1990. 'My grandmother often used to talk to me about the war and how she met my grandfather,' said Fulvio. 'They were soul mates from the moment she walked into the shop at Katzenau – theirs was a really big romance. We will never forget what they endured or the love that brought them together because my Aunt Maria always wears a beautiful gold locket around her neck which contains a lovely picture of Emilio and Elsa kissing.'

ELSA AND EMILIO PICTURED TOGETHER. THEY MARRIED IN 1920.

'Two scrapes with death'
A FAMILY'S FORTUNES IN WAR AND PEACE

The two French soldiers had only been in Robertine Delplace's shop a few moments when a shell hit the building, killing one of them outright and fatally injuring the other. Robertine, aged 19, suffered wounds to her neck; but her sister Beatrice, 24, who was standing with her behind the chocolate counter which took the blast, escaped unhurt. Their grocery shop, however, was destroyed – the windows were blown out, the ceiling came down and all the stock was ruined. As they helped clear some of the debris, the sisters discovered two 5-franc notes covered in the dead soldiers' blood – a macabre souvenir of the shocking event.

All this happened on 23 March 1915 in Vlamertinghe, a small Belgian town near Ypres, which was close enough to the front line that its inhabitants had already started fleeing to France. Robertine's family – her parents Edouard and Emma-Sidonie, sisters Beatrice and Marguerite, aged 23, and brother August, aged 29 – now joined this exodus. They barricaded the doors and windows of their home and what was left of their shop to ensure no-one could get in, and they put up beams to support its damaged frontage. As with many other departing families, the Delplaces had

◀

ROBERTINE WITH HER SONS
GHISLAIN (*STANDING*) AND ADELIN
(*IN ARMS*).

▶

A YOUNG ROBERTINE DELPLACE.

ROBERTINE'S FAMILY'S GROCERY SHOP (*NEXT TO THE CHURCH*) IN VLAMERTINGHE,
DEPICTED IN 1912.

to book their passage to France in advance from Poperinghe station. While they waited for that request to be granted, they stayed temporarily in the small village of Roesbrugge, 13 miles from Vlamertinghe, where their cousin Gery Delplace owned a hotel-restaurant and café called L'Aigle d'Or (The Golden Eagle) in front of a tram stop. Roesbrugge was a busy place and a destination for soldiers taking leave from the trenches. The sisters worked in the café, serving in the restaurant and taking care of the hotel rooms, but these jobs meant that their request to leave was delayed, because the authorities decided there were more urgent cases. Eventually, permission was granted and they travelled to Fresnay-sur-Sarthe, a town 300 miles away in north-west France, where they lived for the rest of the war, with the women staying at home and August finding a job working as a baker. Unfortunately, Edouard Delplace never got the chance to return to Vlamertinghe or to see the end of the war – he fell ill and died, aged 71, on 24 August 1918.

After the Armistice of 11 November 1918, the family went home and were shocked to discover that not only had their house been demolished, but so had the rest of the street. As they waited for their homes to be rebuilt, the locals made use of durable wooden huts that served as living quarters and small businesses, such as

THE CLEAR-UP UNDER WAY IN THE DELPLACES' SHOP,
AFTER THE SHELL BLAST ON 23 MARCH 1915.

cafés, shops and pubs. The Delplaces had owned two other little houses across the street, so they traded this land with their neighbours to give themselves a bigger main plot. While August built a bakery in another part of town, Beatrice opened a shop in a wooden hut on their now enlarged plot, with Robertine providing a bread-delivery service, which proved so popular that she made many friends.

As the shop prospered, a Scotsman called John Simpson Buchan Roy, who had served as a soldier in Belgium, moved next door with his wife Janet, children Ella, Jean and John, and opened Les Trois Soeurs Café. [1] His Vlamertinghe business became very successful, with Roy selling wine, as well as lamp oil and petrol. But on a hot, dry summer's day in July 1921, his luck almost ran out. Robertine's son Ghislain Cornette explained: 'John Roy had been cleaning his motorcycle with petrol on the 31st when he lit a cigarette and the whole thing exploded. His house caught fire and the flames spread to the neighbouring homes. My mother had been sitting on her porch reading her book in the shade when she saw the fire and had to run for her life. It was impossible for her to enter the house because of the heat of the blaze. Her family lost everything but the clothes they wore. John Roy was only partially compensated by the fire insurance company for his losses, so he did not build a new house. Instead, he returned to England and sold his piece of land to my mother and her cousin.' The blaze caused such a stir that the local newspaper, *De Poperingenaar*, reported: 'The fire jumped to the tents next door of the Widow Delplace, shopkeeper, and to the one of Alfons Debruyne. Very few things could be saved. The damage was enormous and only partially insured. Thanks to the very courageous fire brigade of Vlamertinghe, who were on the spot in no time bringing into use their new fire engine, and being helped by many helpful people ... all the other nearby tents and new houses could be saved from the fire. Without this heroism the fire most certainly would have gone further and would have caused more damage.'

After the fire, the Delplace family lived in temporary accommodation, before moving into a new hut. But while they waited for their permanent house to be rebuilt,

A BLOOD-SPATTERED 5-FRANC NOTE BELONGING TO THE FRENCH SOLDIERS
WHO WERE IN THE DELPLACES' SHOP WHEN THE BLAST OCCURRED.

Robertine's mother, Emma-Sidonie, died.[2] Robertine, meanwhile, had fallen in love with Clemens Oscar Cornette, an employee at Vlamertinghe station, and the couple married on 31 August 1926. They lived together in the new house, and Robertine worked as housekeeper for her sister Beatrice. Her first son Ghislain was born in 1930, followed by Adelin in 1932. 'Having overcome the harsh years of war, this was a happy time for my mother,' reflected Ghislain, who still lives in Vlamertinghe. 'I can still remember her talking about the [1915] explosion, but to me being a little boy, she only showed the scars caused by the shrapnel. She spoke more about the [1921] fire because all her souvenirs, documents, photos, clothes and various objects were lost. My mother, who was a very kind and loving woman, had been very lucky to survive two scrapes with death. The family was well-off before the war, but lost a lot of their wealth and that hurt her.' At the age of just 42, Robertine became seriously ill with pneumonia and died a week later, on 24 March 1938, leaving Ghislain, aged 8, and Adelin, aged 6, in the care of their father and aunt, Beatrice. 'The news of her death at such a young age sent a shockwave through the community because she had been a true friend to so many people,' added Ghislain.

Almost 60 years later, Ghislain received a letter from Australia, via the Cloth Hall at Ypres, from an English teacher called Anne Mann. She had been researching her family history and became curious about her grandfather John Roy's time in Vlamertinghe, and about Les Trois Soeurs Café. In his reply (September 1995), Ghislain described the contact as 'a very lucky shot, a marvellous coincidence' and told Anne about her grandfather's accident with the petrol.[3] Anne thanked him for the information, adding: 'With the long history that Vlamertinghe has, I doubt my grandfather was there long enough to be counted. After causing such a dreadful fire, you may not wish to know of him.' She told Ghislain that the Roy family emigrated to Australia in 1924, and John Roy worked as a cellar master and wine blender at Penfolds Wine Company. As for John Roy's children, the letter says: 'The fire obviously didn't change any of the family's habits – all of them smoked most of their lives.'

Endnotes

1 Roy, who was born on 27 January 1879 in Dundee, Scotland, had formerly been a licensee at the Appletree Inn, in Carlisle, England.
2 Emma-Sidonie died aged 70, in hospital in Bruges, on 3 April 1923.
3 Anne Mann, who was living in Burnett Heads, Queensland, and Ghislain Cornette continued their correspondence until January 2005, when Anne sent a Christmas card saying she had been in hospital with a collapsed kidney. Word followed a short while later that she had died.

'Thoughts of a homeward journey'
A CANADIAN'S WAR

Kate Harvey, an English girl from Oxfordshire, was given an empty album on Christmas Day 1901 by her father. By 1919, and having worked at a hospital in Gravesend for five years, she had filled the book with the thoughts and feelings of over a hundred soldiers who had fallen victim to the First World War. The men, from England, Scotland, Ireland, Wales, Canada and Australia, expressed themselves through doodles, cartoons, verses or poems; some penned pictures of their regimental badges, while others simply wrote their thanks. Not much is known about Kate, except that she was born Emily Kate Harvey in the Chipping Norton area of Oxfordshire, in 1876. She died, aged 83, in 1959, and had worked as a domestic help before the war. But, from the sentiments left by her patients, mostly wounded

MONTFORD KERMILLEAU HAYDEN,
IN UNIFORM.

soldiers fresh from the battlefield, it is clear she was well loved. What follows is one of the stories behind a poem in Nurse Harvey's album ... .

When the call went out across the Canadian province of Nova Scotia for men to join the armed forces in 1915, teenager Montford Kermilleau Hayden was among many eager to enlist. [1] Struggling to support his widowed mother, five younger brothers and an older sister, the 15-year-old mill woodworker saw the recruitment drive as an opportunity to serve his country – and more importantly, to bring home a regular wage. The fact that he was two years too young to join up did not seem an insurmountable problem to the strapping 5ft 10in-tall youngster. Instead, he lied about his age, telling the recruiting sergeants he was 17, and to make identification even more difficult he went by his unusual middle name, 'Kermilleau'. But the claims aroused suspicion, and his mother, Edith, was asked by the authorities to confirm that her son was old enough to go to war. Knowing how desperately he wanted to enlist, she went along with the fabrication, and without confirming when he was born she wrote a letter in November 1915, which said: 'Dear Sir, At the time of my son's birth there were no certificates used, so am enclosing now a birth card filled in to give you his correct age. Also have had it signed by Pastor of Baptist Church here. Trusting this may prove satisfactory to you. From Mother of M.K. Hayden, Yours truly, Mrs Edith M. Hayden.' In his note to confirm Mrs Hayden's claims Reverend J. Harry Puddington of the Springfield Baptist Church, wrote: 'To whom this may come, this is to certify that the named soldier M.K. Hayden's birth – it is as stated by his mother – is correct.' The ruse paid off, and within a year Private Kermilleau Hayden, of the 85th Nova Scotia Highlanders, found himself on board RMS *Olympic*, the sister ship of the unfortunate *Titanic* which had hit an iceberg and sunk only four years earlier. The *Olympic*, a White Star transatlantic ocean liner, had been chartered by the Canadian government in 1916 to transport up to 6,000 troops per crossing from Halifax to Europe – a five-day voyage that made many soldiers sea-sick.

It was four months after he disembarked in Liverpool, on 18 October 1916, that Kermilleau's active service began in France. However, much of his time was marred by injury and ill health. In October that year he was hospitalised with an injured right leg; by December he had been admitted five more times, in Rouen and then in Buchy, suffering from the effects of shell gas. On 6 April 1918, Kermilleau transferred to the 4th Battalion Canadian Machine Gun Corps, which was formed in March 1918, becoming part of the 4th Canadian Division. Even his attempt at two weeks' leave from France, in June 1918, resulted in his being returned to a war hospital in Leith,

Scotland, with influenza. But it was in September 1918 that Kermilleau suffered his most serious injury. His daughter Mildred Hayden Morrison said: 'He told me that he and his buddy were together firing at the enemy when a bullet ricocheted off his machine gun, striking his finger, hitting his buddy and killing him. The bullet had hit my father on the right hand, almost severing his middle finger.'[2]

It is very probable that Kermilleau sustained his wound when involved in the assault on the Drocourt–Queant Line – a heavily-fortified system of trenches and shelters that formed part of the northern sector of the Germans' much-vaunted Hindenburg Line, which ran from Arras to Laffaux in north-eastern France. Between 2 and 3 September 1918, the 1st and 4th Canadian divisions led the charge, smashing through the line and inflicting heavy losses on the German army. It was a crucial phase in the Allies' Hundred Days Offensive that would eventually lead to victory. Kermilleau's war records show that he was admitted to Chatham Military Hospital, Fort Pitt, Kent, on 5 September 1918, with a gunshot wound to his right hand. The wound was dressed before he was transferred to Princess Patricia's Canadian Red Cross Hospital in Bexhill, Sussex, for his finger to be amputated. However, a poem attributed to Kermilleau in Kate Harvey's album suggests that he also stayed at Gravesend Hospital – possibly Knock Hill Lodge, Gravesend, which was affiliated to Chatham Military Hospital, 10 miles away. His pay certificates support the suggestion that he was in Gravesend, because while he was there he made two small payments, almost certainly to buy tobacco.

THE LETTERS FROM KERMILLEAU'S MOTHER AND THE BAPTIST PASTOR,
WHICH ENABLED HIS UNDER-AGE ENLISTMENT.

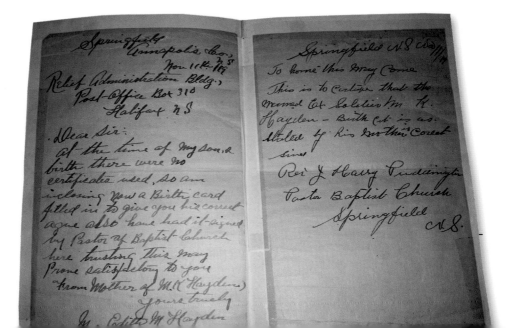

The three verses in his poem, written on 25 September 1918, speak quite positively about marching past fresh green fields, whistling as he goes, but dreaming of the day when he and his colleagues can march home. Kermilleau's daughter, who read the words for the first time in 2012 after her own daughter, Leslie, discovered Kate's album online, said she did not recognise the writing as her father's, even though it is signed 'Private M.K. Hayden', with his service number 223320 and unit, the 4th Canadian, Machine Gun Battalion. It is also unlikely that he would have been able to use a pen so soon after losing his finger. However, Mildred believes he probably had the poem written down by a nurse. 'Seeing it just blew me away because it struck me as just the kind of thing he would say. When you read it to yourself, it sounds just like him. When I was a child he would often talk in poems to me and my mother; usually a funny poem he made on the spot for a situation. I expect my father had this written down as his way of expressing himself. After all, his colleagues were able to write home to their wives and children, while my father, at that time, didn't have a family of his own. It was just marvellous to have stumbled across this almost 100 years after it was written.'

> *There's a wide highway before us*
> *And the fresh green fields around*
> *With just and song we swing along*
> *To the drums inspiring sound*
> *We may be fighting to-morrow*
> *Yet never a bit we care*
> *And we hump our packs on aching backs*
> *And whistle a martial air*
> *Thoughts of that homeward journey*
> *Will help us to dare and do*
> *And we'll speed the day, when with music gay*
> *Our dreams march home come true*
>
> *No 223320*
> *Pte M.K. Hayden*
> *4th Can, Machine Gun Batt*
> *September 25th 1918*
> *Canada*

NURSES, AS DEPICTED IN A SOLDIER'S SKETCHES FROM KATE HARVEY'S ALBUM.
THEY WOULD HAVE BEEN A VERY FAMILIAR SIGHT TO KERMILLEAU.

It would appear that Kermilleau did not return to the war after his injury. As he waited with his colleagues to be demobbed, he was admitted in December 1918 to the No. 9 Canadian General Hospital at Kinmel Park, Rhyl, in Wales, with a 'typical attack of appendicitis pain, tenderness over McBurney's point, vomiting on two occasions.' He underwent an appendectomy on 13 December and was discharged a month later, allowing him to join his comrades on 1 February 1919 for the voyage home aboard RMS *Carmania*, one of the fastest liners in the Cunard fleet. The ship had been converted into an armed merchant cruiser during the war, before being tasked with transporting Canadian troops home.

Within months of his return, Kermilleau met his future wife, Jennie Elmira Veinot, during a chance encounter in Bridgewater, Nova Scotia. 'My mother was actually engaged to someone else at the time and had been out enjoying a festival weekend with her best friend in Bridgewater,' said Mildred. 'While they were there, they went to see a fortune teller who told my mother: "You're going to walk over a bridge and meet the man you're going to marry." The only way home was to go over a bridge, and who should my mom meet, but my father. She broke off her engagement immediately and she and my dad were married a year later in 1920.'

The couple had a daughter, Elizabeth, in 1921, but moved to Massachusetts, United States, two years later, where Kermilleau found work as a house builder and building inspector. They went on to have their second daughter, Mildred, in 1927. 'My father was a great guy, extremely popular and outgoing and could tell stories endlessly,' said Mildred. 'I was a bit of a tomboy and spent a lot of time with him hunting and fishing. He never talked about the war, but when my children asked him how he'd lost his finger, he'd tell them that it was after he'd battled with a tiger. He would also rest his cigar in the gap between his fingers. My father received a pension from the Canadian government for the loss of his finger, and I can remember in the 1980s three men from the pension board coming to his house to give him his war medal and offer him a higher rate because he was the longest living disabled war veteran at that time. He refused the offer, saying he and his wife were doing well enough.' In fact, Kermilleau and Jennie were married for 69 years, and according to their family were a devoted couple.

Armistice Day always had a special significance to Kermilleau; it was a date given extra poignancy by his passing, on 11 November 1990, aged 90.

Endnotes

1 When Britain declared war on 4 August 1914, the Dominion of Canada soon sprang to arms. Thousands of men responded to the call; by the end of the war, Canada recorded 211,000 casualties, 152,000 of them wounded and more than 50,000 of them killed.

2 Mildred Hayden Morrison, who lived in Cape Cod and helped so much with this story, passed away on 30 August 2013, aged 85.

'Our ship's gone down'
THE STRANGE DEMISE OF LORD KITCHENER

As gale force winds and rain lashed their cottage in the early hours of the morning, Mary and William Phillips, and their 19-year-old daughter Mina, were woken by the sound of a knock at the door. Outside were two soaking-wet sailors who told them: 'Our ship's gone down – we need help! There are more that could be saved.' The exhausted pair – Richard Simpson and Jack Bowman – told how they had been on board the armoured cruiser HMS *Hampshire* when it blew up and sank, off Birsay, at the western edge of Orkney's principal island, Mainland.[1] 'They were bedraggled and exhausted after coming off a life-raft in rough seas,' said Mina's son Jim Sabiston. 'They managed to get up a cliff and went to the nearest house, which belonged to my grandparents who had been unaware of the tragedy. It would have still been light, so easy for them to see the house. My grandparents got the fire going, made them tea and something to eat, before putting them to bed. My

mother said the lads were so different in their attitudes; while Jack was grief-stricken, saying "oh my poor chums," Dick said: "Aren't we lucky, Jack?" My grandfather went out with the neighbours to search the beaches for more survivors. He managed to rescue three boys by going down the cliff with a rope tied around his waist, with the other farmers holding on to the top. But he was stopped by the authorities who told them it wasn't their place to do this – they were very disappointed.'

◄

RICHARD SIMPSON IN HIS
NAVAL UNIFORM, COMPLETE WITH
HMS *HAMPSHIRE* HATBAND.

According to locals, a number of similar rescue attempts were thwarted, some at gunpoint, by naval men who said they did not need civilian help, and who even ordered the Stromness lifeboat, which had prepared to launch, to stay in port or face a charge of mutiny. It was a decision that many claimed was partly responsible for the huge numbers of lives lost that stormy night of 5 June 1916.

The official naval report stated that 643 men died while only 12 survived; but some historians believe the casualty numbers were far greater. However, what few would have known at the time was that the dead included a very important figure: no less a man than Lord Horatio Herbert Kitchener, 1st Earl Kitchener of Khartoum – an illustrious imperial hero and since 1914 Secretary of State for War, whose finger-pointing image and commanding appeal succeeded in persuading huge numbers of volunteers to enlist. Earlier that day he had boarded the ship on a secret diplomatic mission to Archangel, Russia. He was travelling to meet the Russian Tsar, Nicholas II, in order to boost morale and improve relations between the two Allies. Before he joined the fateful voyage, Kitchener had shared a meal with Admiral Sir John Jellicoe, commander of Britain's Grand Fleet, aboard his flagship HMS *Iron Duke*. There he heard Jellicoe's account of the Battle of Jutland which had ended just days earlier, with both sides claiming victory. [2]

By early evening, Kitchener had boarded the *Hampshire*, and despite fearsome weather the ship set sail from the Grand Fleet's Orkney base at Scapa Flow escorted by destroyers HMS *Unity* and HMS *Victor*. The appalling conditions slowed down the two smaller vessels and they were forced to turn back, leaving the *Hampshire* to continue alone into a Force 9 gale. At around 7.40pm, when the *Hampshire* was only 1.5 miles away, between the islet of the Brough of Birsay and Mainland's Marwick Head, an explosion rocked the 11,000-ton cruiser, and she sank within minutes. The ensuing drama was witnessed from land by 11-year-old John Fraser, from Feaval, Birsay, after his father told him to watch 'this big battleship passing in these rough seas'. He told BBC Radio Orkney, in an interview seven decades later: 'Almost immediately a cloud of dark smoke rose from the water's edge, followed afterwards by a huge explosion and a tongue of flame shot out round the gun turret in front of the foremast ... Immediately they steered her for land, turned her straight in, and we thought "Oh, he's going to beach the ship," but it was no time 'til she turned round again, I suppose, with the force of the north wind and the heavy seas ... By this time her bows were down in the water and her ... propellers were clear of the water, and she just slowly went down, and the bows slowly went down until it seemed to us to

WAR SECRETARY LORD KITCHENER BOARDS JELLICOE'S FLAGSHIP HMS *IRON DUKE*,
5 JUNE 1916, FOR WHAT WOULD PROVE HIS LAST LUNCH.

hit the bottom, and the stern just settled down in the water. In all, I think it was just 15 minutes until she disappeared beneath the water.'

In a letter from the Phillips' cottage to his mother in Tynemouth, Richard Simpson detailed how he and a number of his crewmates battled to escape the sinking ship on a 'Carley' life raft, while others perished in the perilous seas. [3] 'We were about three miles off the shore when the ship blew up and it was the most terrible sea I have ever seen, you could not get any boats into the water, and if you had, they would have been instantly swamped, so I stood by a big float along [with] another 50 or 60 people and when the order came we launched her. We had the terrible four hours in the water as you can imagine; seas mountainous-high washed over the top of us. Anyway, we started to drift towards the shore, which we reached more dead than alive. We had to swim the last few yards because it was all rocks and we were lucky to escape the rocks in which there were thousands and we got ashore and climbed up the cliff after falling three or four times. We found a cottage belonging to a farmer of which there are about six, and it is from there that I am writing this letter. The people are very kind to us, giving us clothes, eggs, bed, everything we need. I forgot to tell you. Out of the sixty that started, six of us were alive when we reached the shore, the same with the other buoy. Only six out of sixty survived here and that makes twelve. We expect to leave Wednesday, when this letter will be posted. On the shore beside the house there are hundreds of dead bodies. Well dear, I am in the best of health and spirits. We lost everything as the ship went down in twenty minutes. Well I expect to see you in a week's time, or a fortnight. I expect we will go to Barracks. I want you to keep this address for me as it is the people I am staying at.' He signed the letter, 'Your loving son, Dick'.

Kitchener's death caused shockwaves around the world. In London, the news was met with amazement and incredulity. As word spread like wildfire across the city, newsboys were mobbed by crowds eager to learn the facts; the government's War Council was summoned – of which Kitchener had been a key member and flags were lowered to half mast. It was believed that the *Hampshire* had hit a mine laid by a German submarine at the end of May, but before the Battle of Jutland. However, subsequent inquiries into the tragedy revealed that intelligence reports suggesting mine-laying activity in the area by submarine *U-75* had been ignored, and that Jellicoe had failed to pass on the warnings to Kitchener at their lunch.

Kitchener's body was never found. Survivors claimed that he was last seen on the bridge of the *Hampshire* and had been unwilling to board a life raft. However, the circumstances surrounding the death of one of the most popular public figures of the time, and the scuppered rescue attempts, led to numerous conspiracy theories as well as local resentment. Tom Muir, from the Orkney Museum, said: 'People believed all sorts of things; that the government organised to get rid of Kitchener, that the IRA were involved, that there was gold bullion on board and that the ship had been sabotaged by a German sympathiser in revenge for his family being persecuted by Kitchener's troops in the 1899–1902 Boer War.' He added: 'This was a tremendous disaster for the Royal Navy – Kitchener was a huge hero in the eyes of the public, although that was not an opinion shared by his Cabinet colleagues. They had just had the humiliation of the Battle of Jutland and then a few days later the war secretary, who is trusted to their care to go to Russia, is lost. He doesn't even leave Orkney – he only gets up the coast a couple of miles and dies. But the real question is: why the authorities refused help from local people and in some cases physically drove them back at gunpoint? There was a feeling that more lives could've been saved if they had listened to local fishermen, whose lives depend on the sea, who

HMS *HAMPSHIRE*, FROM WHICH RICHARD SIMPSON WAS ONE OF ONLY 12 SURVIVORS
AFTER SHE STRUCK A MINE AND SANK ON 5 JUNE 1916. KITCHENER WAS NOT SO LUCKY.

knew all the tides and currents around that coastline, where the rafts would come ashore, and who were the best placed to help. Some of the bodies they found were still warm because they had climbed the cliffs but been unable to hang on because of the cold and just dropped off into the sea. The people felt insulted and couldn't help but believe there was something suspicious going on.'

However, Orkney war historian Brian Budge thinks confusion and incompetence, rather than conspiracy, was a more plausible explanation for the local military's decision to prevent civilian intervention, because it was unlikely many people would have known Lord Kitchener had been on the *Hampshire*. He does believe, though, that wartime chaos, along with ineffective communications, affected the accuracy of the casualty figures released in 1916. He claims that 728 people are known to have perished in the disaster – 85 more than the number officially declared – following his research into Commonwealth War Graves Commission registers, which reveal that among those unaccounted for were Kitchener himself, Munitions Ministry officials, clerks, a driver, servants and even a detective. [4] 'The navy meant well and put out a casualty release to let the families know as soon as they could, but even if there were mistakes, people didn't question them because the war was on and there were other priorities,' he said. 'After all, men were going on and off ships all the time – for leave or assigned to other ships – so the numbers were fluid. Unfortunately, when a ship goes down, often the best records go down with it.'

The tragedy had such an impact on Orkney's people that they raised money to have a tower memorial to Kitchener built on Marwick Head. It was dedicated in 1926, and one of the observers present was Richard Simpson's mother, Christina. She kept in touch for many years with the Phillips family, who had given him shelter, but she had a more poignant reason for being there too. Some 13 months after her son's dramatic escape, the young able-seaman was killed when his ship, the steamer SS *Thames*, was sunk by the German U-boat *UC-63* off Grimsby on 14 August 1917, with the loss of ten lives. He was aged just nineteen. His niece Kathleen Stewart, who has recently renewed ties with the Phillips family, said it was a tragic end to a short life. 'It's really sad that after being one of only 12 survivors from the *Hampshire*, after scrambling up a cliff side to safety, he then returns to the sea and dies,' said Kathleen. 'My dad [Richard's younger brother, Thomas] was very proud of Richard and I can always remember seeing a plaque to him on my grandmother's wall, along with a photo of the *Hampshire*. What I didn't know was that there was such a friendship between my grandmother and the Phillips family, and that she had been up to Scotland. It was only recently we discovered how important it all was – that my uncle had survived an ordeal that had led to the death of a war hero. His letter home must've given my grandmother so much hope, yet just over a year later, and like Kitchener, his life was finally claimed by the sea.'

Endnotes

1 The story of Richard Simpson was contributed by the Tynemouth World War One Commemoration Project.
2 The Battle of Jutland was the biggest naval battle of the war, fought on 31 May and 1 June 1916 in the North Sea waters off the coast of Denmark. On the face of it, the Royal Navy came off worse, losing more men and more ships; but the damaged German High Seas Fleet never ventured out in full force again – until it surrendered.
3 'Carley' float – a lightweight life raft made from a long tube of copper bent into an oval ring and covered with waterproof canvas. The floor was made of slatted wood. It was designed by American inventor Horace Carley and supplied to warships during both world wars.
4 The exact number in Kitchener's party aboard the *Hampshire* can never be known. The names of the main officials are known, but the servants with them were not all recorded. The 643 figure used in most accounts was in newspaper reports based on the Royal Navy's press release at the time, which described the ship's complement as being 655, of whom only 12 survived.

'It saved my life'
A CLOSE ENCOUNTER ON THE SOMME

Lieutenant William Andrews and his sappers had been working through the night building a machine-gun emplacement in the ruins of the newly retaken French village of Contalmaison when a blast blew him off his feet. The 23-year-old Irishman's helmet took the full force of a piece of flying shrapnel, smashing a four-inch gash from rim to crown and knocking him unconscious. As William lay on the ground, still dazed but unmarked and strapped to a stretcher, he heard a young soldier suggest they throw away the battered headgear. Outraged, William, a lieutenant in the 128th Field Company of the Royal Engineers, called out: 'Give it here to me – it saved my life – I want to preserve it for my grandchildren.' With that, he was taken away, along with his helmet, to a nearby field hospital.

It was 11 July 1916, early in the Battle of the Somme. The Allied offensive, which continued from 1 July to 18 November, was a major British and French assault on the German lines in Picardy, which resulted in over a million casualties among the combatants. By 10 July, after days of hard fighting, the British 23rd Division – part of General Sir Henry Rawlinson's Fourth Army – reached Contalmaison, three miles north-east of the town of Albert. As soon as the infantry confirmed that the village had been taken, William and his sappers were called in to consolidate the advance. 'My father was in charge of the construction of a machine-gun emplacement and setting up barbed wire defences in no-man's land,' said his son Michael Andrews. [1] 'This was in full view of the enemy and could only be carried out under cover of darkness. It is arguably the most dangerous situation on the whole field of battle; only a charge across open ground against enemy entrenchments would have involved greater exposure. It was during these operations that he was struck by shrapnel.'

For William, who reported back for duty 18 days later, it was a lucky escape following a year of active service in France. The fifth of nine children, he was born in 1892 to schoolteacher Mary Ellen O'Neill and William Andrews at Omagh Gaol, where his father was acting governor. The gaol, which was the scene of several hangings, was in particular famed for the 1873 execution of Thomas Montgomery, a police inspector who was tasked with investigating the murder of a bank employee – when in fact Montgomery was the perpetrator of the crime. When the gaol closed

SECOND LIEUTENANT WILLIAM ANDREWS, 1915.

in 1902, the Andrews family were separated temporarily, with William senior transferring to a posting in Cork with some of his children, while Mary continued her work in Omagh with the rest of the family.

By 1913, William, who was living with his father, had graduated from University College, Cork, with a degree in civil engineering. He was working at various construction sites in Scotland when war broke out, and prompted by a sense of adventure, a persuasive war propaganda campaign and a lack of work he volunteered for the British Army in 1915 and was commissioned to the Royal Engineers. He was enrolled on an Officer Training Course, taught to ride horses and sent to the front line

WILLIAM (*FRONT ROW, SECOND FROM LEFT*), NOW PROMOTED CAPTAIN, 1917 – POSSIBLY IN MESOPOTAMIA OR ON A SHIP.

in France. 'My father was an extrovert and full of self-confidence,' said Michael. 'That, allied to real quick wittedness and decisiveness, made him ideal officer material.'

On 25 April 1917, William was awarded the Military Cross by King George V at Buckingham Palace. His family know little about the act of gallantry in the face of the enemy that prompted the award, except that he was admired for his coolness in leading the way out of the trenches. [2] However, his time in France was short-lived. 'After more than a year at the front, including involvement in the frightfulness of the Battle of the Somme, he contracted pleurisy and had to be invalided back across the Channel to England,' said Michael. 'He became very sick and was in real danger of dying. He was moved from one hospital to another, finishing up in a major London hospital under the care of a Harley Street specialist. By the time he was discharged, he had lost half of one of his lungs and faced breathing problems for the rest of his life.' William was deemed 'unfit for active service', which meant that he could not return to the trenches and was instead destined for an office-bound job at a supply depot near London. 'He told me the work was desultory, routine and absolutely meaningless,' said Michael. 'He found it intolerable after the critical, life-and-death role he had played in the trenches. He requested to be sent back to his unit in France, but that request was refused. Instead, inexplicably for a man with only 75 per cent of his lungs left – in less than perfect condition at that – he was sent to Mesopotamia to fight the Turks in 1917.' William remained in Mesopotamia – now Iraq – until the war was over. Even the journey to get there was gruelling, involving three months at sea to reach Basra, followed by 300 miles overland. 'It is clear my father arrived at the front in "Mespot" long after the 1917 advance had stopped with the capture of Baghdad,' said Michael. 'He saw the Battle of Sharqat from a high vantage point – the last battle of the campaign, late in 1918.' [3]

When it was his turn for demobilisation in April 1919, and by now a captain, William was delighted to be offered a commission in the regular peace-time army. 'This was a considerable compliment because only a tiny percentage of the huge wartime army could be offered places,' said Michael. 'It was also a secure livelihood in a Britain where prospects of employment for returning soldiers were bleak.' When his posting came, it was to Ireland, which at first seemed like a dream come true. 'However, when he realised that he was to be part of an army being sent to Ireland to suppress the continuing unrest which followed the 1916 Rising and became the War of Independence, my father said it was impossible for him to undertake to fight against his own people, so he had to turn it down.' [4] He resigned, resumed civilian life

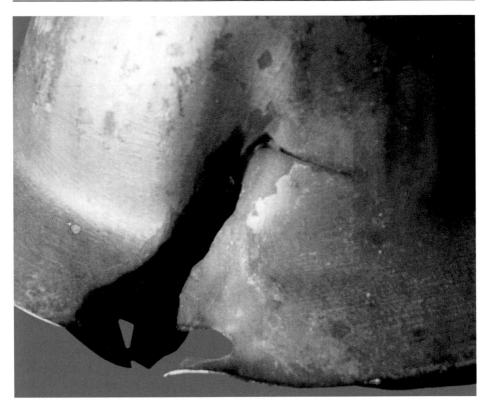

WILLIAM'S HELMET, SHOWING THE SHRAPNEL DAMAGE.

in Ireland and eventually returned to work as a civil engineer some 18 months later. His job took him all over the UK, including to London, where he met his future wife, Christina McAleer, a civil servant, also from his home town of Omagh. The couple, who married in 1923, returned home to have a daughter, followed by three sons.

As the Second World War got underway, William was persuaded by a brigadier who had commanded him in the earlier war to rejoin the army as a lieutenant colonel. However, his hopes of being part of the campaign in Egypt were thwarted by army doctors, who deemed him 'unfit for active service'. Instead, he was posted to Northern Ireland where he oversaw the construction of several large camps built for Americans based in the province. His efforts resulted in his receiving the Bronze Star Medal – one of the most highly regarded awards the US military could present to individuals for bravery or acts of merit or meritorious service. After the war he became head of the roads division at the Cement and Concrete Association in London, and probably because of his success with the Americans he was chosen to join a fact-finding mission to the United States in 1948. The transatlantic trip, which was to look at future road-building techniques, also gave William the opportunity to contact many of the Americans he had met during the war. However, the lung problems he suffered in the trenches were never far away. He suffered a racking and frequent cough, which was exacerbated by his smoking habit, and by 1957 he underwent an operation at St Bartholomew's Hospital in London to remove cysts from his lungs. The procedure put a strain on his heart and he was left very weak. William and his wife retired to Greystones, County Wicklow, where he regularly played bridge, chaired the local tennis club and enjoyed visits from his six grandchildren. But in 1960 his health took a turn for the worse. His second lung was congested with cysts and surgery was the only option. 'He was pessimistic about the outcome of further surgery because he had been so near death the time before,' said Michael. 'He knew the risks only too well, but decided to face up to them and agreed to the operation. The outcome was almost inevitable; he died three days later aged sixty-eight.'

William was buried at Greystones, and it was another 30 years before he was joined by his wife, Christina. 'The truncation of my father's life was a little tragedy – certainly for him,' said Michael. 'It can be looked upon as the price he paid for surviving the war. Had the shrapnel struck an inch or two higher he would have been killed. Had he not contracted pleurisy, it is very likely he would have become another battlefield casualty. In the end, his life was claimed by the illness that saved him from an early death. His story is just one example of the potential that was wiped out by the war to end all wars.'

Endnotes

1 At the time of writing, William Andrews' son Michael and his grandson Vincent Murphy were producing a book about the man and his helmet.

2 Citations for the Military Cross were published in the *London Gazette* during the First World War. However, if the MC was a King's Birthday or New Year award – and William's award was in the New Year's Honours List – details were not published and in most cases are not available.

3 Mesopotamia – dubbed 'Mespot' in soldiers' slang – was a loosely governed part of the Turkish Ottoman Empire. Fighting commenced there as early as November 1914, as soon as Britain went to war with Turkey. Despite early reverses, the British and Indian forces, by now commanded by Lieutenant General Sir Stanley Maude, were making significant progress by early 1917. The Battle of Sharqat (23–30 October 1918) was the final encounter. It concluded when the Armistice of Moudros ended fighting across the Turkish Front.

'No More War'
BROTHERS IN ARMS

They were brothers in blood and brothers in arms, and – according to loved ones – Albert and Jeroom Hebbelinck could not have been closer. From the moment their mother Maria died, shortly after Albert was born in 1895, the pair shared an unbreakable bond. While their father, Joannes Baptista, continued his work as a wholesale dealer of office materials near the family home in Ghent, Belgium, the day-to-day care of his three sons Raymond, Jeroom and Albert became too great a burden, so Albert was taken on by a childless aunt and her nobleman husband, the squire Tayart de Borms. During their teenage years, Jeroom was dispatched to a military training school in Kortrijk (Courtrai), while Albert was enrolled at the renowned boarding school, the Lycée d'Anvers in Antwerp. Despite being separated by over 60 miles, the brothers stayed in constant touch by postcard, according to Albert's son, Jean.

By the time war broke out in August 1914, Jeroom was 21 and Albert 19, and the pair eagerly joined the Belgian army together. 'Like many other young adults, they were immediately ready to enlist voluntarily and defend their fatherland with enthusiasm,' said Jean. 'They saw the war as an adventure that would not last long, so they grabbed it with both hands while they could. Going to the front, they sang: *Vive La Guerre!* [Long Live the War!], but they soon changed their tune. When the first wounded and amputated soldiers returned from the battles, they realised the awfulness of the situation. They did not sing anymore – that was something my father told us repeatedly.'

Just two months into his army training, Albert was transferred to the 1st Battalion

◀

ALBERT AND HIS BROTHER JEROOM, ON LEAVE IN
PARIS, SOME TIME BEFORE JEROOM'S DEATH IN 1916.

of the 2nd Infantry Regiment, fighting in the Battle of the Yser, which took place between the towns of Nieuport (Nieuwpoort) and Dixmude (Diksmuide), and which was part of the Germans' attempt to break through and reach the Channel ports of Calais and Dunkirk (Dunkerque). By this time most of Belgium was in German hands, and the Yser, a narrow river that runs into the North Sea near Nieuport, was the last natural border on Flemish soil. Keen to retain this last vestige of his country's territory, Belgium's King Albert deployed all the army at his disposal to defend the front and the nation's reputation, declaring: 'You will find yourselves alongside the gallant French and British Armies. Our national honour is at stake. Face to the front in the positions in which I shall place you, and let him be regarded as a traitor to his country who talks of retreat.'

The German offensive began on 18 October with a heavy bombardment of the Belgian lines. For several days the Belgians, reinforced by 6,000 French Marines and an infantry division, fought back, using the embankments of the Yser and the Nieuport–Dixmude railway as their lines of defence. On the night of the 21st, the Germans slipped quietly across the Yser at Tervate. By the 25th, the situation was becoming so desperate that the Belgians took the decision to flood the area between the river and the railway. The sluices were opened at Nieuport on 26 October during high tides, and the low-lying ground east of the railway started to flood. By the 31st an impassable area of water was created, stretching as far south as Dixmude, forcing the German army to abandon the idea of crossing the Yser. Dixmude only fell on 10 November 1914, extinguishing the last Belgian and French stronghold on the river's right bank; but the Belgians' bravery in flooding the plain meant that they were able to hang on to a small, narrow piece of home territory throughout the war, thus restoring national pride and in turn making their king a national hero.[1]

For almost two years, Albert fought in the trenches unscathed; but his brother Jeroom was not so lucky. He had joined the 10th Company of the 2nd Infantry Regiment – the same as his brother – and on 1 July 1916 was killed by a rifle bullet to his chest at Kaaskerke, a district of Dixmude. Albert's son Jean said: 'My father was devastated by his brother's death. Not only had he lost his best friend, he was starting to see the senseless nature of war. It was a turning point for him – one that would influence the rest of his life.' Just three weeks after the tragedy, Albert was admitted to hospital in Steenkerke. Jean described how two years of being in muddy, wet, slippery trenches with ill-fitting boots had taken their toll on Albert's feet. It is likely that he was suffering from 'trench foot' – a condition caused by the cold, wet,

ALBERT HEBBELINCK
(*SEATED, FAR LEFT*), WITH
OTHER VETERANS OF THE
YSER, DURING THEIR
RHINELAND DUTY, 1919.

insanitary conditions, which if left untreated could turn gangrenous and result in amputation. But ten days later Albert was back in his regiment, and three weeks after that he was posted to the 1st Battalion of the Army Cyclist Corps, part of the Cavalry Division. The cycling units were employed as scouts on enemy positions, as couriers in communication trenches, and as security patrols. ² According to Jean, Albert used to cycle towards the German lines and report on their positions. It was during one of these missions on his Raleigh bike that he was almost killed by an explosion. Jean described it: 'He was hit in the chest by a piece of shrapnel, and was saved by his shaving razor which he kept in his breast pocket. The razor case was damaged, but it took the force out of the shrapnel and stopped it going into his heart.'

Albert was punished on a number of occasions during his war service, receiving six days' detention for being at the front as an observer without a rifle, and just over a week for wearing inappropriate attire in the trenches. He was held for a further eight days in a police cell in July 1918, after he was found more than six miles away from his billet despite having been refused permission to leave. After the Armistice, Albert was among the occupying forces guarding the Rhineland in Germany. He was demobilised from the army in 1919 with a skin condition that left him covered in boils. 'My father said the food at the front was miserable, mainly canned food, such as a kind of American corned beef,' said Jean. 'As a consequence, he developed deep abscesses. Nothing seemed to get rid of them; but being an ardent reader he started to search for natural remedies. Together with the advice of a health food practitioner, he decided to become a vegetarian, eating a great deal of raw plant-based food. The result was surprising: within a few months he was completely healed and it was the start of him adopting a completely healthy lifestyle. Not only was he a vegetarian, he was also a non-smoker and a teetaller.'

In 1920 he married Henriette De Backer, aged 21, and they went on to have three children. The couple became members of the Seventh Day Adventist Church, where Albert used the platform to share the basic principles of a healthy lifestyle. In 1928, he founded NATURA, the first health food store in Flanders, to promote healthy living. He always went cycling during his summer holidays and brought up his children as vegetarians.

His grief over his brother's death and his altered views about war also prompted him to join the Vlaamse Oud Strijders (VOS, meaning 'Flemish Old Warriors'), a veterans' organisation that espoused veterans' rights and the Flemish cause. During the war, Flemings in the army had campaigned against the imposition of French, as spoken by Belgian Walloons, as the single language officially in army use. After the war, and adopting the broken-rifle symbol and slogan 'No More War', VOS members became increasingly pacifist, protesting against any manifestation of militarism. [3] However, part of the movement went on to collaborate with the German occupying forces in the Second World War, and some members even joined the SS to fight for the Nazi regime on the Eastern Front, which left Albert disillusioned. He quit the VOS. 'Having seen what war had done to people and how it had taken his beloved brother from him, my father would have no truck with anyone who wanted to promote it further,' said Jean. 'It led him to raise his three children in a spirit of pacifism and with an anti-militaristic attitude. We were never given fake weapons to play with, and my father passed on his negative attitude towards military training to us all. In the Second World War I refused to carry arms and was posted to the administrative section. Even my brother Marcel, a university graduate, shunned officer training for an admin job, to avoid having to fight.'

Endnotes

1 Peter Barton's *The Battlefields of the First World War*, 2005, sums it up nicely: 'For the next four years the great man-made sea, 13 km long and 6 wide (8 miles long and 3 wide), was kept in place, and never again were the Germans to set foot west of the railway.'

2 The use of bicycles for communication and reconnaissance work was invaluable. Unlike horses, bikes were easier to handle, quieter, more economic, lighter and did not require feeding. They could also cover fifty miles a day with a package attached.

3 The first Yser Tower, a memorial on the Yser at Dixmude, was built by Flemish nationalist war veterans, who had not forgotten the inequalities of having been led by French-speaking officers whom they could hardly understand. Today's rebuilt tower, 84 metres high, is inscribed *AVV – VVK*, i.e. 'Alles Voor Vlaanderen – Vlaanderen Voor Kristus' (All for Flanders – Flanders for Christ). It remains a symbol of Flemish nationalism, but also pacifism, carrying the demand: 'No More War' in Dutch, French, English and German.

'At a great risk of life'
AN UNLIKELY FRIENDSHIP

To outside observers, Bernard Darley was a quiet, modest man whose world revolved around his children, the Catholic Church and his work as a jeweller. Yet, a small brass matchbox kept by the family for almost 100 years gives a clue to another side of Bernard's personality. Born in 1886, the only son of caretaker Stephen Darley and his wife Mary Ellen Darley (*née* Hoben), Bernard grew up in Birmingham, where he became a jeweller in the city's Vyse Street – part of the historic Jewellery Quarter in Hockley. He was still working there when war broke out in 1914, but it was not until 1916 that the father of three enlisted as a 'Second Class Air Mechanic' in the Royal Flying Corps, forerunner of the Royal Air Force.[1]

According to his records, Bernard did not go overseas until after the war, when, as a Leading Aircraftman (LAC) and Fitter (motor transport), he was sent from RAF Uxbridge to an airbase in St Omer, Northern France. The site, which had been used as the main British air base during the four years of fighting, was the hub of a huge behind-the-scenes operation, involving thousands of technical staff sent to repair everything from planes to wireless equipment and vehicles. It was during this postwar clearing-up operation that a fire broke out in a power station at the workshops on

3 September 1919. Fearful lest the heat would cause tanks containing oil and petrol above the building to explode, Bernard sprang into action with a German Prisoner of War Otto Arndt. Together the pair ran into the burning building to put out the blaze, which also threatened to set fire to high-voltage electricity cables. A letter from Bernard's captain, commending his 'act of gallantry', described how: 'No. 28345 LAC Darley, B. was assisting with a fire extinguisher and attempted to enter the burning building, but owing to the intense heat, was unable to succeed. After

◀

BERNARD DARLEY, IN THE SERVICE DRESS OF
THE ROYAL FLYING CORPS, *c.*1917.

playing on the fire for a few minutes, this airman again attempted to enter the building and this time was successful. With a fire extinguisher he fought the fire from inside the building, and after a time was able to reach the window and took hold of the hose which was handed from the fire engine ... LAC Darley was assisted through the whole operation by German Prisoner of War No. 585 named O. Arndt of the 139th POW Company. The act of entering the building

THE MATCHBOX MADE FROM SHELL CASING, WHICH WAS GIVEN TO BERNARD DARLEY BY GERMAN P.O.W. OTTO ARNDT.

was done at a great risk of life owing to the fact that immediately above the burning building are two tanks, one filled with petrol and the other with oil. These might have burst at any moment owing to the intense heat. There was also great danger owing to the fact that, in the power station were exposed live electric wires carrying current of 15,000 volts.' A further letter sent on behalf of the wing commander in charge of the RAF in France and Flanders noted that Bernard took 'a great personal risk'.

According to his family, this act of bravery forged an unlikely friendship between Bernard and Otto Arndt. 'As a token of their time together, Otto created a little matchbox out of a brass shell case,' said Bernard's grand-daughter, Merilyn Jones. 'On one side he hand-carved "St Omer" and on the other, "Souvenir from France". The little box and the memory of that dramatic incident meant the world to my grandfather. He was such a gentle, modest man he never talked about the war or what he did – he left that to my mother. When I think of my granddad and Otto running into a burning building at great risk to their own personal safety to put out the fire, it makes me feel very, very proud.'

Bernard died in 1948, aged 62. Sadly, attempts to trace Otto through official records were not successful, because his date of birth was never recorded.[2]

Endnotes

1 According to Bernard's service records, he was engaged by the Royal Flying Corps on 13 May 1916 and was transferred to the RAF when it was formed on 1 April 1918.
2 There are records of a goldsmith called Otto Arndt, born in Rathenow, Germany, in 1897, who served in the Luftwaffe during the Second World War, but it has not been possible to confirm whether he was the same man that Bernard knew.

'A couple of francs per bottle'
ADVENTURES OF AN UNDER-AGE RECRUIT

Private Arthur 'Slim' Simpson and his comrades had only just settled into their billet – a French barn behind the lines – when they were thrown out by their superiors. 'The sergeants came along and said: "Out of here – we'll have this," so we had to go down to a cellar.' Using charcoal's faint glow to light the room, Slim said he was not bothered about the new accommodation and instead turned his thoughts to making his colleagues a stew. 'We found a load of peas and flour, and when our rations come up, a bit of meat; I thought we'll have a bit of a feed,' he said. To the initial disgust of his fellow soldiers, he cleaned up an enamel chamber pot to cook the meal in, and placed it on a brazier in the cellar. 'When they came back I said: "We've got some nice food for you tonight." To which they replied: "In that?!"' 'Yes, it's all right,' he said. However, before the food could be served, one of the men knocked over the stove and all the straw on the floor caught alight. As they busily stamped out the fire and swept up the mess, to their astonishment they found a secret door. 'We pulled the trap door up and there's a cellar there and there's miles of bottles of wine and all sorts of things and barrels of it,' he said. Slim said the soldiers drank some of the alcohol, and in the morning when their sergeant came round for an inspection he

realised they were drunk. Slim tried to explain the incident away by saying he had managed to get hold of a few bottles of wine during a stroll through the village; but his claims only made the sergeant more curious about the source – and whether he could have some too. 'I'm not going to tell you – you'll be round there, won't you?' said Slim. 'I said: "We'll get you some – you can have it for a couple of francs per bottle – but we don't know what it

◄

SLIM SIMPSON AFTER THE WAR. HE ALWAYS
WORE GLASSES, WHICH HE CLAIMED
WAS AS A RESULT OF A GAS-SHELL ATTACK.

is. You've got to take what it is." "That's all right; we'll have a couple of bottles."' After the deal was done, Slim said he took a circuitous route around the village a number of times because he was sure the sergeant was following him.

For several days, the alcohol-selling arrangement continued until an officer approached Slim and said: 'I understand you've found some wine or something?' Slim replied: 'Oh no, not our chaps,' whereupon the officer responded: 'It's all right – you don't want to worry – we could do with some ourselves.' Slim answered: 'We don't know what it is – it's all sorts; there's no label on it. You can have it the same as the sergeant – a couple of francs a bottle.' In Slim's recollection, 'we got a few bob in the kitty – a few francs – we couldn't spend it, but it was there.'

It was only when his company was set to move up the line that Slim finally admitted where he had been getting his secret stash. 'The sergeant said to me: "Where did you get that stuff? You know we followed you all round the place. Where did you get it?" I said: "I'll tell you now." We knew we'd never come back there again – and even if we did come back there, we wouldn't go to the same place, so I said: "You know that place you slung us out of, and you took our billet over and made us go in your cellar? It was in there." He said: "No, it wasn't – we went down in that cellar." I said: "Well, we had a bit of an accident. We tipped the brazier up and set fire to the straw, and when we were clearing up the straw, there was another cellar under there – and that's where the wine was." He said: "No wonder we couldn't find it when we followed you around."'

Slim's secret wine-cellar story was one of many funny, fascinating and poignant tales he told his friends and family over the years following the war. Born in 1899 to Herbert Simpson, a drayman, and his wife Minnie, who worked as a dressmaker, Slim was just 15 years old and living in Lambeth, South London, when war broke out. [1] He got fed up with being teased by girls in the street who believed that he was older than his years and should be serving his country; as he was already working as a motor mechanic, he decided to volunteer as a driver. However, while his tall, slender frame – which led to his nickname – easily fooled his peers that he was mature enough to sign up, it took a while longer to convince the numerous recruiting officers that this was the case. In an interview recorded more than 60 years after the war, Slim laughed heartily when he told how he visited all three services several times in an attempt to enlist. It was only after he had almost given up hope – aged 17 – that he was finally accepted on 23 August 1916, by the 6th (City of London) Rifles. [2] His older brother, Herbert, was already serving with the 20th (County of

London) Battalion at Blackheath and Woolwich. However, Slim's A1 medical record ruled him out of the driving job he sought; instead he was deemed fit enough to fight, so he trained as a Lewis gunner.[3]

According to the National Roll of the Great War, Slim, who later served in the 2/17th London Regiment, saw action at the battles of the Somme, Amiens, Bapaume and in other engagements during the retreat and advance of 1918.[4] He had only been in France for three days when he was ordered to go over the top, and at the same time witnessed the death of two friends. He was injured several times during more than two years in the field. On one occasion he suffered problems with his eyes after he could not get his respirator on fast enough following a gas-shell

THE OLDER SLIM, PROUDLY WEARING HIS MEDALS FROM THE 1914–18 CONFLICT

attack, while he was carrying rations up from the base camp. On another occasion his ear was damaged by a piece of shrapnel, and his wounded colleague was killed while they were on their way to a dressing station. When a German then jumped out of a trench covered in blood, Slim feared he had stumbled into enemy lines. 'I thought, "Oh Christ, I've gone the wrong way back." Instead of that, he had his hands up. I said: "Are you wounded?" "No". "Do you speak English?" "Yes." He'd been a waiter in London for years,' said Slim. The German, who was covered in his dead comrades' blood, helped Slim down to the dressing station, where he was bandaged and dispatched to the 5th Canadian Hospital in Rouen. Slim said he had expected to be sent home to Britain, but so many stretcher cases arrived that he was taken back up the line.

In one of his many anecdotes, Slim told how he and a colleague washed using water from a shell hole – something they were advised against because of the risk of contamination – only to find, when it dried up, that there were three dead enemy soldiers at the bottom of it. He collected so many buttons, badges and souvenirs from the ground for his belt that his waist looked like 'a brass foundry'. He claimed he had no hatred for his German 'enemies', describing them as 'quite good people' and 'good fighting men', although he said his opinion might have changed had he known earlier about how his brother Herbert, a signaller, died on 12 June 1918 after he became a POW. Slim said the War Office had informed the family that his death had been as a result of dysentery and general weakness during captivity. However, he was later told by one of his brother's mates, who was also held with him, that he had been 'hit over the head with the butt of a rifle' by one camp official, while another 'shoved a bayonet into his chest and finished him' following an altercation with a German padre who was rude to him – a story that was confirmed years later by a fellow soldier from the 20th London at a British Legion gathering. Herbert is buried in Glageon Communal Cemetery, near Cambrai. [5]

After the war, Slim joined the Army of Occupation in Germany and was demobbed in October 1919, having earned Wound Stripes, and the British War and Victory medals. Postwar, he took up work as a painter and decorator, before meeting dressmaker Gladys Letchford. The couple married in 1926 and moved into a house owned by her brother in Lambeth. Slim was 40 when the Second World War broke out, and because of his injuries he was unable to fight. However, he signed up with the Balloon Squadron in August 1939 and flew barrage balloons on Clapham Common to stop enemy fighters from getting at London.

Slim's great-niece Valerie Richards described him as 'a lovely man, very friendly and very kind. The First World War was obviously the most important thing that ever happened to him – and that's why he never stopped talking about it. To him it was life in its fullest range, with horror, humour, fear and boredom everything you could imagine. I got the impression it was the most alive he ever felt.' [6]

Endnotes

1 'Drayman' – a man who earned his living from delivering beer on a horse and cart (dray)

2 Slim's enlistment date is confirmed on a ticket entitled: 'Movements from concentration camp to embarkation camp'.

3 'Lewis gun' – a light machine gun, operable by one man, which could be mounted on a prop or a parapet/ledge for firing, and in use with the British Army from 1915.

4 A clothing slip to be attached to a dispersal certificate states that Slim was in the 2/17th London Regiment.

5 The National Roll of the Great War also mentions Slim's brother, Private H.E. Simpson, who joined up in March 1916, fought in operations on the Somme and was wounded. He received 'protracted medical treatment at Manchester Hospital and on recovery returned to France and was in action at the Battle of Cambrai. Taken prisoner during the German Offensive in March 1918, he died whilst a prisoner of war on June 12, 1918.'

6 Valerie Richards added that Slim 'never held a grudge, except against the people involved in his brother's death. He was a Royal British Legion delegate for over 50 years and he and Gladys organised trips around the graveyards in France and Belgium every Easter for their annual holiday. While he and Gladys never had children, he was the one we youngsters always wanted to see because he was the most fun. It was the reason why we taped the interview with him – we were lucky to have him and we thought it would be nice to share him and his experiences.'

'The fire had burned so fiercely'
RISE AND FALL OF A PRODIGY

Dr Hermann Ernst Watzl had always known he would be famous. As a young ambitious man, born in Austria in 1889 to a military family, and educated at the University of Heidelberg, his brilliance as a chemist was recognised very early on. He was just into his twenties when the Austrian government saw his potential and chose him to work in the United States, learning about new inventions and devices that could be used in warfare. By 1913 he was living in Cleveland, Ohio, and had met and married Marie Cahill, an attractive graduate from the city's Case Western Reserve University. For Ernst, a monocle-wearing, heel-clicking workaholic, life in America was on the up. However, with the outbreak of war in 1914, his American dream had to be put on hold and he was called back to Austria.

While Marie stayed in Vienna, where she gave birth to their daughter Herta, records suggest Ernst became a lieutenant in the No. 4 'Klagenfurt' Regiment of the *Gebirgsinfanterie* (Mountain Infantry), which later fought in the harsh climate of the Alps on the Italian Front.[1] Photographs taken by Ernst show that during rest and relaxation periods he went swimming with his colleagues in Lake Levico, close to the military zone, where he was even visited by his wife and child. Reports claimed that Ernst went on to become captain of a flamethrower unit; however, his photos suggest it is unlikely that he saw any frontline action and rather that he was employed to train specialist soldiers on the use of flamethrowers against Italian troops. The weapons, which were invented by German engineer Richard Fiedler, worked by launching burning fuel at

◄

ERNST WATZL AND HIS WIFE MARIE DURING
THE FIRST WORLD WAR.

►

MARIE AND THEIR DAUGHTER HERTA VISIT
ERNST WATZL AT THE FRONT IN
THE SUGANA VALLEY, IN TRENTINO.

SOLDIERS WATCH A FLAMETHROWER IN ACTION,
IN A PHOTOGRAPH FROM ERNST WATZL'S OWN ALBUM.

the enemy through a lit nozzle, either from a portable gas cylinder strapped to the back of the operator, or from a larger, more static model whose range was twice as far. Flamethrowers were used to clear enemy soldiers from their front-line trenches, but just the sight of them was often enough to frighten troops away. The results were terrifying, intimidating and shocking for anyone caught in the flamethrower's path, and were equally perilous for soldiers handling the device, who risked being killed if the cylinder exploded, or faced certain death from an unforgiving captor if they were taken prisoner. According to John Stark Bellamy II, who has written about Ernst's postwar life, he was very proud of his involvement in the flamethrower unit. Ernst even told a Cleveland meeting of the Army Officers Association in 1928 how he had demonstrated the weapons to Germany's Kaiser Wilhelm II who, along with his entourage, was dressed in an asbestos suit.[2] However, the images of the devastating aftermath of flamethrowers, with victims charred beyond recognition, must have stayed in his mind forever.

After the war, Ernst returned to his scientific work, and another daughter, Jane, was born. However, the siren call of the United States never left him, and in December 1924 the family of four boarded the passenger ship SS *Columbus* at Bremen, in northern Germany, bound for New York. Returning to Cleveland, Ernst became an expert in the purification of water and a member of Watzl-Schweitzer Inc., a water filtration company. Accordingly, his new processes were sought by water works across the country, so it was no surprise to his wife when he told her he was going to Philadelphia on 27 October 1929, in pursuit of a lucrative position as a consulting engineer and to sell his invention to city officials. He borrowed $5,000 as he left, ostensibly to secure the position. It turned out to be the last time Marie would ever see her husband. On 6 November, his car was torched on the banks of the Schuylkill River, near Pottstown, Pennsylvania, and was discovered by police the next day. 'There wasn't much of it left: the fire had burned so fiercely that its glass windshield, windows and instrument panel had completely melted, and much of its steel frame had been fractured by the heat,' notes Bellamy in his book. 'There was no trace of a driver or passenger in the ruins of the car, but, disquietingly, there was a set of distinct footprints leading right into the Schuylkill River ... and not returning. It looked bad, and the discovery of four suspicious-looking cans in what was left of the back seat immediately suggested to the Pottsdown and Royersford police that the fire had been spurred by an accelerant.'

Investigators explored several theories about the crash, ranging from accidental death to foul play. However, several new developments pointed to Ernst still being alive. His life insurance premiums were still being paid by an unknown source, and police discovered that he had been maintaining a studio-office in Cleveland. There he had been employing Mrs Mary Horvath McGranahan, a pretty young secretary and model who disappeared shortly after the car incident, prompting her husband to sue the Austrian chemist for $50,000 for the estrangement of his wife.

The mystery was solved, however, within a few months. On 24 March 1930 reports came through that Dr Ernst Watzl, aged 41, and Mary McGranahan, in her early twenties, had been found shot dead and penniless at the Hotel Sacher in Vienna. The couple, who had checked in as Johann Flassak and wife four days earlier, had secretly wed in December 1929. A medical examination revealed Ernst had shot Mary before turning the gun on himself. It was believed that they died before midnight, the point when Ernst's life insurance premiums would have expired. According to suicide notes found at the scene, Ernst admitted faking the car accident in Pennsylvania so his wife and two children would get the insurance money. In a letter to a friend published in the *Huntsville Daily Times* on 26 March 1930, he said: 'Knowing the custom of insurance companies, I realised that any wife would be unable to cash my policy of $35,000 unless she could establish my death officially. But I also know that the claim would fail if my premiums were not paid regularly to my death. Then I remembered the insurance instalment falling due tomorrow which I am unable to meet. Thus my wife will be robbed unless I die today. I am therefore going today, before the premium is due.' He also revealed his relationship

THE OLDER ERNST, COMPLETE WITH MONOCLE, IN CLEVELAND, UNITED
STATES, 1928. HE HAD JUST BEEN OUTLINING A NEW CHLORINATION
PROCESS, WHICH HE CLAIMED WOULD GIVE CLEVELAND PURE WATER.
BY COURTESY OF THE CLEVELAND PRESS COLLECTION, MICHAEL
SCHWARTZ LIBRARY, CLEVELAND STATE UNIVERSITY.

with his secretary and where he had been after the accident at Pottstown. 'I first went to New York where I bought a false passport in name of Flassak and secretly married Mary McGranahan. Fearing recognition, we determined to quit New York, which we did, and went to Canada. In Canada we were nearly caught so we decided to go to the coast and take a steamer across the Pacific. We did so, sailing to Tokyo, where I hoped to find a job but quickly realised there was not [a] chance. So we went to India. Here we bought jewellery and trinkets, which will be found in our luggage. Leaving India we went to London but pushed on to Vienna. But the $5,000 I took from my bank at Philadelphia after my automobile escapade was soon eaten up. We were faced with two alternatives; either to go to my parents and relatives and ask assistance or to commit suicide. I preferred the latter.'

Vincenzo Cali, whose daughter Elisabetta is married to Ernst's great-grandson, said: 'Ernst's story is fascinating because it just makes you want to know: "Why?" What made him change from being a sensible, disciplined military man to a fugitive who then went on the run across the world with a woman who wasn't his wife?' John Stark Bellamy II said he believed Ernst's upbringing in the Austro-Hungarian Empire, together with his family's military pedigree and schooling, had all played a part in his self-destruction. 'It seems likely too that his exposure to the horrors of World War I had its wonted demoralising impact on him,' he said. 'The result was a deeply conflicted man, who desired personal satisfactions that couldn't be reconciled in his deeply divided and obviously guilt-wracked psyche: the settled, respectable bourgeois realm with wife and children and the thrills of sexual/romantic fulfilment offered by an apparently willing, attractive and worshipful young woman. And while Watzl may have been a particular and peculiar product of his place and time, his tragedy is really just another illustration of one of the world's oldest stories: the middle-aged man throwing away his life for the allure of a younger model.'

Endnotes

1 The elite *Gebirgsinfanterie* Regiment No. 4 'Klagenfurt' was part of the Austrian standing army, the *Landwehr*. It was hurriedly brought back from fighting Russia on the Eastern Front when Italy unexpectedly abandoned its neutrality in May 1915, joined with the Allies, and declared war on Austria-Hungary – though not yet on Germany.

2 John Stark Bellamy II is the author of six books and two anthologies about Cleveland crime and disaster, one of which, *The Killer in the Attic*, includes the chapter 'The Man With the Twisted Life' detailing the life of Ernst Watzl.

'I knew it was my turn'
WOUNDED ON THE SOMME

As dawn approached, with it came the strangled gasp of 'Jack' Stafford's friend. 'Following his gaze I saw hundreds of grey clad Germans advancing from the front and on both flanks,' said Jack. 'We were in a bottle neck! The covering party in front was cut off; and not a word has been heard of them since. We stood our ground for a while and then the order was given to retire. But the enemy was almost on us from three sides and the nearest cover to which we could retire was half a mile away. A hunted look flashed across the face of my unnamed companion to my left – I judged he was looking to me for a lead, so I hastily joined the others. I had only moved 20 yards when "crack", the bullet had found its home. I was pitched forward and with the thought drumming through my mind "I knew it was my turn", I cursed my luck at being "preyed" at such a disadvantageous spot.' He had been shot in both legs.

It was 8 August 1916, and John Stafford – always known as 'Jack' – had been at the front for 18 months. He was a private with the 5th Battalion (Territorial Force), King's (Liverpool) Regiment. Just days before, when his battalion had been ordered to cross a dangerous strip of land known as 'Death Valley' to a position in front of Trones Wood, the 20-year-old soldier had been overwhelmed by the feeling that his luck was about to run out. It was a premonition that many of the soldiers involved in this, the Battle of the Somme, might have experienced. [1] This critical offensive, launched on 1 July, was intended to be a decisive breakthrough by the Allies along 20 miles of the front either side of the River Somme, in Picardy. It was also supposed to draw German troops away from battering the French at Verdun. Notoriously, by the end of that first day, the British Army had suffered the worst loss for any day in its history, with 60,000 casualties, of whom almost 20,000 were dead. It is a record that still stands, and the battle as a whole would go on to consume over a million casualties on all sides.

▶

JOHN STAFFORD IN UNIFORM.

POSTCARD FROM JOHN STAFFORD TO HIS MOTHER, 1915.
JOHN IS AT THE EXTREME REAR OF THE PHOTO, SHOVEL IN HAND, TO THE LEFT OF THE
CENTRAL FIGURE WITH THE COAT AND CAP. THE CARD IS DATED 2 JANUARY 1915.
IT IS QUITE POSSIBLE THE MEN WERE BEING TAUGHT THE CRAFT OF 'TRENCHING'.

As Jack considered his own sense of foreboding, he also knew that, being a 'water carrier', it was vital that he transport two petrol tanks of the stuff to his section, along with his usual full load – ammunition, two Mills bombs, two Very lights and iron rations. [2] 'I conjectured how long it would take to reach the dressing station from my present position,' he wrote in his memoirs 20 years later, contemplating what might happen were he to be wounded. 'Some miles of winding communication trenches would have to be traversed; Death Valley would have to be crossed, to make no mention of the constant rain of shells that were exploding over the affected area. If my wound or wounds should render me a stretcher case the outlook was worse. Nevertheless, I wished for that something to happen there and then.' Jack reached the fringes of Trones Wood with the water intact, and stayed there for a day and a half. At midnight on August 7/8, the company was ordered to advance, after a scout reported that there was no sign of the enemy for at least 600 yards in front. 'I had now no desire to be hit for the danger of being taken prisoner loomed ominously,' Jack recalled. 'My belief, though, was as strong as ever.'

But on 8 August, as he set about providing cover for himself and his pal, Jack's

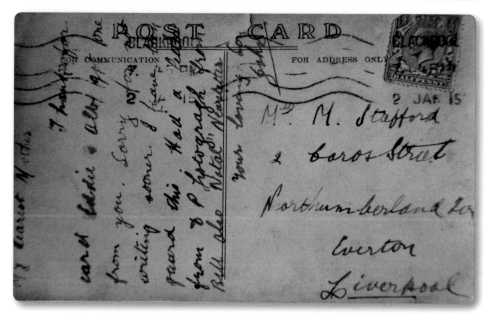

REVERSE SIDE OF POSTCARD TO JOHN STAFFORD'S MOTHER

apprehension about being hit was realised. He was felled by a bullet that passed through the flesh of his upper left thigh while also entering the extreme inner high point of the right leg. 'Here I lay 20 yards from the Germans, scared to move for fear they would spot me and either make further movement impossible or take me prisoner,' he said. 'A look about did not bring within sight any shell hole into which I could crawl at a favourable opportunity and in which I could remain till the cover of darkness, about 16 hours hence. I knew that one of my legs was twisted like a corkscrew – and the other, though burning feverishly, was fairly sound as I could bend the knee and twinge my toes. I did not try to move, so the extent of possible progress was unknown to me. The crackling of German rifles, which had been deafening, had ceased. I reasoned there were no more targets to aim at. Then followed the thud of spades – the Germans were strengthening the position. I could hear the noise of their voices, though I could not understand one word of their talk. I did feel slightly relieved to know that they were consolidating as I was satisfied they would advance no further and their lookouts would not be so alert, thus giving me the chance of crawling towards the British lines, unseen.'

It was at that moment Jack spotted a British soldier moving very slowly ahead of him: 'At all costs I must keep Tommy in sight, I thought, and when at a safe distance from the Germans, I would call him and he would give me a helping hand.' [3] After moving about 15 yards, the Tommy disappeared into a hole. Jack fixed his eyes on that spot and moved forward, though the pain of shifting his badly smashed right leg over irregular ground was, he said, 'indescribable'. Eventually he fell into a narrow trench about 20 feet long, 3 feet deep and some 2 feet wide. 'I might have landed in the trench head first, but on recovery, I discovered that my badly injured leg was screwed half way up my back; the foot of the other leg touching the extreme end of the trench. The voice I heard was that of the Tommy from whom I had hoped to receive a helping hand. He was in a sitting position at the other end of the trench and I could only gain view of him by looking backwards over my head as it was impossible for me to sit up. What a terrible sight – he had unbuttoned to tend his wounds and was in the act of using his field dressing. Poor fellow, no wonder he called for water; he had two terrific wounds in the stomach. For this reason he had moved so slowly before. For this reason his legs dangled when he had disappeared from my sight.

'There was a little water in my bottle, but my equipment was bundled under my back and it was some considerable time afterwards that I managed to procure the water bottle. The calls for water were not of long duration – Tommy groaned and groaned. I spoke to him, but could not get a reply. He, like myself, was unable to move. I could not take my eyes from him, though it strained my neck to look at him from my awkward position.'

'I watched that poor fellow die and was not able to comfort him in any way, except prayer. Slowly his knees moved upwards and his chin tilted downwards 'til the end came and he toppled forward and remained in the position of an Easter worshipper at prayer. How strange he looked; his clothing had slipped down over his head, and his back, which showed the two points at which the bullets had entered, was exposed skywards ... No, I would not die!'

'The belief that I should survive the war was strong within me. But I was very weak; my thirst was terrible. I commenced the task of extricating the water bottle from my equipment and at the same time endeavoured to straighten my right leg. Perhaps after a drink I should feel stronger and get my leg into some shape I could move a little. My thoughts were, of course, that I could creep away when it was dark and make for the British lines.'

After examining his wounds, Jack found his gaze returning to his dead companion.

▶

JOHN STAFFORD AND HIS
WIFE MOLLIE, AFTER HE WAS
AWARDED THE M.B.E.

'What a peculiar attitude!' he wrote. 'Now I could not see his face at all. Even prior to his death I only secured a contorted view of his face which I was unable to recognise. No word had passed from his lips other than the few pitiful calls for water. I knew all the men of my Company, except those of a draft recently arrived from home. He must have been a new man. I continued to gaze at him and an abundance of thoughts passed through my mind – his mother, his father and so on and so on.'

Jack's thirst increased with the heat of the day; his leg burned and shells burst all around him, causing his head to throb and the smell of explosives to sicken him. Using his elbows he tried to drag his body along, but the effort was exhausting. 'This was no doubt due to the loss of blood which had been flowing freely from both legs for some hours,' he said. 'The ground on which I lay was completely red; the upper part of my trousers and the lower back portion of my tunic were a corresponding colour. I knew that to move by my own effort was out of the question, but I also knew that I would not share the fate of my companion. I knew I would survive the war!'

But as the hours passed, the sun sank low and his thirst heightened, Jack watched, mesmerised at how the German Very lights cast 'their greenish brilliance over the corpse of my companion, thus making his figure more ghoulish and grotesque than ever'. He said: 'And so that night with its thousands of memories passed. My helpless weakness, my thirst, the burn of my wounds, the nip of the night air, the quiet periods, the sound of German voices, the blinding flash from the explosion of a nearby shell, the vicious crack to the German rifles, the devilish pranks of the Very lights, the grotesqueness of my dead companion and my unanswered optimism. Yet NOBODY HAD FOUND ME!'

By sunrise Jack discovered that his wounds were infested with maggots, which explained why they had burned so intensively. 'Occasionally I looked at their swelling rhythm then finally turned away in disgust,' he said. Eventually drowsiness overcame him; but then he woke with a start and the feeling he was being suffocated or buried alive with cold water trickling down his neck. 'My senses gradually recovered and I heard friendly voices. "Where are you hit chum?" I had been found! What a glorious feeling ... It was still very dark and I could not see anybody, but I felt a pair of hands under my armpits. The voice continued to talk. "What mob are you?" I answered: "5th Kings". "Oh, we relieved your mob yesterday. I'm in charge of a reconnoitring patrol. No idea we were so near to Jerry's lines. Up went a Very light and we dived into this strip of trench for cover. My pals are just behind me. You've emptied their water bottles. You fairly put the breeze up us when you yelled."'

'It seems one of them jumped on me when they scrambled for cover and I yelled. A friendly Very light had revealed I was a Tommy. The pluck and kindness of that corporal and his colleagues I shall never forget. The corporal remained with me and sent his pals for a stretcher, urging them to hurry as dawn was approaching. Luckily, the night was pitch black.' Jack told the corporal about his companion and asked him to recover his pay book and personal effects. 'He seemed anxious to be away from that unfortunate body,' said Jack. 'As it was still dark he could not ascertain the dead man's name – and to this day I am in ignorance as to his identity.'

Finally the stretcher arrived. 'How those fellows risked their lives that I, already half dead, might live. They struggled over uneven ground for about a mile, lowering the stretcher and laying flat themselves whenever a Very light shot into the air. In fact, the latter part of the journey did not give them the protection of darkness as dawn rapidly approached and they carried on completely exposed to the Germans. When they reached the British Front Line, the stretcher was most tenderly lowered to the foot of the trench and everybody seemed anxious to add some form of comfort. I remember little from that point until I arrived at the Advance Field Hospital Station.

The doctor looked at my wounds, covered me up without placing on any dressing, and tacked to my tunic a green label on which was written "maggots". I was borne back across "Death Valley" feeling very groggy, vaguely remembering my inward journey across this valley, but feeling very conscious of my fulfilled presentiment.'

After almost two years in hospital recovering from his injuries, Jack entered the Civil Service as a clerk, working in the Army Records Office, firstly in Liverpool, and then at Fullwood Barracks in Preston. He was permanently disabled and had to wear a surgical boot, because his right leg was 3.5 inches shorter than his left. Jack continued his work with the Army Records Office during the Second World War, and was posted to London during the time when the German Blitz was pounding the city, in 1940–1. He was awarded the MBE in 1946, and died in Preston, in 1959.

It was when Jack had been off work in 1936, attempting to learn to write with his right hand after suffering writer's cramp in his left, that his wife Mollie suggested he practise by working on his war memoirs. 'I can remember him sitting and writing for hours, thinking "what are memoirs?"' said his daughter, Joan Almond. 'I read them for the first time a few years ago and I was so overcome with emotion I had to put them down. My father was a very gentle person and he didn't talk about the war. But I can imagine the trauma of watching that other young soldier die and being absolutely unable to help him at all would have been something that haunted him for the rest of his life – more than his own injuries.'

Endnotes

1 Wilfrid Miles, in *History of the Great War: France and Belgium, 1916*, Volume II, London, 1938, pp. 177–8, records the circumstances of 8 August 1916: 'At 4.20 am on the 8th August the infantry went forward. There was an easterly wind and considerable mist, and the whole field of view was further obscured by dust and smoke, the German artillery having put down a heavy barrage. Visual signalling was out of the question and for a time no runners got back ... The line, mostly shell-holes, reached by the 1/5th King's was out of touch on both flanks: it represented the sole British gain of the day.'
2 'Mills bombs' were types of grenade, standard in the British Army from c.1915 and designed by William Mills. 'Very lights' were flares, normally projected from a special pistol, to signal or to illuminate the battlefield at night, and developed by the American naval officer Edward W. Very (1847–1910). 'Iron rations' were (often tinned) food carried by a soldier for emergency use. The standard iron rations, according to the British Field Service Pocket Book of 1914, weighed in at 2lb 6.5oz and consisted of biscuit, preserved meat, tea, sugar, salt, cheese and meat-extract cubes.
3 'Tommy' – a private in the British Army, as derived from 'Thomas Atkins', a generic name given in examples of how soldiers should complete army paperwork.

'Are you a good swimmer?'
A PERILOUS ESCAPE

As he rushed into her parents' café in Berendrecht, north of Antwerp, Paul Bouvette's words tumbled out in French. The dark-haired young man in his twenties told Maria Christine Van Meir he was from the southern Belgian town of Mons, was fleeing the Germans and risked being shot. He desperately needed to get over the border into Holland and he needed help fast. According to Maria's son, her first reaction was: 'Are you a good swimmer?' She told Paul the border with neutral Holland was closed by a 2,000-volt electric barbed-wire fence and was guarded so strictly that his only means of escape would be to swim down the River Scheldt into Dutch territory. If he thought he could swim that far, she would meet him that evening when the tide was low and help him get away.

MARIA CHRISTINE VAN MEIR AND HER FAMILY.

It was 18 July 1917, and Belgium – except for a small portion of Flanders – had been occupied by the Germans for almost three years. In 1914 Winston Churchill, Britain's First Lord of the Admiralty, had attempted to bolster the Belgian King Albert's resistance in Antwerp; but the attacks on the city were so overwhelming that the king, along with the army and thousands of residents, had had to retreat over a pontoon bridge on the Scheldt. It was the start of an exodus, which saw a million Belgians escape to Holland and 500,000 more to Britain and France. While many of them returned during the war, fearful of losing their homes to the German occupiers, others were making their way out of occupied Belgium to fight with their king and the Allies at the front. In a bid to stop this 'illegal' traffic via Holland, the Germans built a 9-foot high electric fence in 1915, which stretched for more than 190 miles between Belgium and Holland. It was a dangerous obstacle but one that many people managed to conquer – by using wooden sash windows and casks to force their way through the entanglement, or by going over the top using ladders placed on either side. However, not every attempt to overcome the barrier was successful – by the end of the war the lethal current had claimed the lives of many hundreds of people.

To the 27 year-old Maria, who had taken pity on the young Paul, scaling the fence was not a safe option. Instead, the pair kept their rendezvous at the café, which was two miles from the Scheldt. However, to reach the river they first had to find a way past a fort occupied by German soldiers who knew Maria and her father: he was the local blacksmith whose services they used for general forging requirements. To divert attention away from themselves, they agreed to pretend they were boyfriend and girlfriend. 'They walked towards the river arm in arm just like a young couple,' said Maria's son Louis Van Gysel. 'When they arrived at the fort a German guard said: "Look at the blacksmith's daughter with her sweetheart," to which my mother whispered back: "Don't tell my father!" and he let them go.' When the pair reached the river, Maria helped Paul hide in a haystack and left him to wait until nightfall and low tide. As soon as it was dark enough he slipped into the water and started to swim downstream. 'Paul was in danger the whole time because the current was very strong and he risked being picked up by German searchlights from the bank,' said Louis. 'He was in the water for about two hours when at last he heard the sound of oars. He thought he'd been spotted by a German patrol boat, but then he heard a person swear in Dutch, so he knew he was safe. He had been found by a Dutch fisherman in a rowing boat who helped him out of the water and took him ashore

MARIA (*SECOND LEFT*) WITH PAUL BOUVETTE
(*LEFT*), LOUIS AND ANNE MARIA AT THE REUNION
IN BERENDRECHT IN 1969

near Ossendrecht, Holland, about five miles away.' As soon as Paul was settled, he managed to get a postcard smuggled into Belgium to tell Maria their plan had been a success. On it was the coded message they had agreed at the riverbank: 'Charlotte arrived safely, but she's got a cold.' 'My mother could've been shot for what she did – she was unbelievably brave,' said her son Louis.

While Maria knew that Paul had made it to Holland, she heard nothing more until 1925 when his mother, along with his sister, visited Berendrecht asking after the girl who had helped her son to safety. The parish priest took the women to see Maria, who was by now married with two children, but still living in the village. 'As soon as Paul's mother saw Maria, she said: "You have saved a priest of the Lord,"' said Louis. 'Paul had returned to Mons and became a Jesuit priest. My mother was overjoyed to hear he was safe and back home.' Maria, who had married Achille Van Gysel, the deputy manager of a sugar factory in Berendrecht after he returned from the war, went on to have seven children. When the factory closed in 1930, Achille started a bakery and café in front of the village church. By 1937 the family decided to move to Antwerp, where they took over a café, restaurant and hotel in the city centre. However, their happiness was short-lived, because Achille became ill with cancer and died in 1943, aged 52, leaving Maria with a business to run and seven children aged between 8 and 19 to bring up.

During the Second World War, Maria's eldest daughter, Juliette, was captured and imprisoned by the Germans for six weeks for wearing a little badge in the Belgian colours of black, yellow and red, which bore the words: 'Keep Smiling'. Her eldest son, Edmond, was sent to a re-education camp near Leipzig, for refusing to work for the Germans. 'When Antwerp was liberated on September 4, 1944, my mother, big-hearted as she was, opened her home to the tired soldiers so they could have a bath, clean up, have some food and nightcaps,' said Louis. However, the loss of Antwerp and its port facilities was a major blow to the Germans, who in their revenge blasted the city with V-1 and V-2 missiles.[1] The worst of these attacks proved devastating for

Maria, because her 17-year-old son George was killed, along with 566 others, when a V-2 fell on the city's Rex cinema on 16 December 1944.

Years later, when Maria was talking about her experiences in the First World War and the story of Paul Bouvette, she began to wonder whether he was still alive. Keen to find out, Louis's wife, Anna Maria, went to see the Jesuits in Antwerp, who discovered that Paul was still living in Mons. They made contact, and in 1969 Paul was reunited with Maria more than fifty years after they had first met. 'As soon as Paul saw my mother, he thanked her for saving his life,' said Louis. 'We all went to Berendrecht and my mother and Paul linked arms, just as they did in 1917, to visit the spot by the river where he'd entered the water. It was very moving to see these two old people reliving the past together, arm in arm. Paul confirmed my mother's story in every detail, just as she had told it to us – there was absolutely no exaggeration.'

Maria spent the last years of her life living with her youngest son Theo and his wife until she died in 1976, aged 86. However, even after her death Maria had a revelation for Louis and his wife. In 1979, when the couple were on a trip to Doel, on the Scheldt, visiting the birthplace of Louis's father, they struck up a conversation with two men. 'To our great surprise they told us my mother had hidden them from the Germans at her hotel for two months. This wasn't easy because the hotel had been partly occupied by Germans. None of us children ever had a clue – our mother had taken this secret to her grave.'

Louis, who lives in Wilrijk, near Antwerp, added: 'My mother was a very courageous woman. When danger came her way, she didn't run; she handled it. She helped people escape the enemy in both wars, but to her it was just normal – if someone needed her help, she did what she could to give it to them. Her life and her actions make me very proud to be called her son. She was truly a person to look up to, and all these years later, I still do.'

Endnotes

1 The V-1 flying bomb, also known as the 'Buzz Bomb' or 'Doodlebug', was essentially a small pilotless aircraft with a warhead and a range of 200 miles, which emitted a droning sound until it fell to earth and exploded. The V-2 was a rocket – a ballistic missile – carrying over a ton of high explosive, whose speed and height of travel gave no warning to its victims and made it virtually impossible to intercept. London and Antwerp were the principal cities targeted in the Nazi campaign in 1944–5, until the launch sites were either destroyed, overrun or forced back out of range by the Allied advance.

'I am in Munich'
A MESSAGE FROM HITLER

Dear Lanzhammer
I am now in Munich with the depot battalion. Currently I am under dental
treatment. By the way I will report voluntarily for the field immediately.
Kind regards
A Hitler

The sentiments on this postcard from Munich are so ordinary
– yet the writer of them went on to become the most reviled dictator of the 20th
century.[1] Adolf Hitler had been recuperating in Munich, after being seriously injured
by a shell fragment, when he wrote this message to his friend Karl Lanzhammer. The
27-year-old Lance Corporal Hitler had been sheltering in a dugout during the Battle
of the Somme, in October 1916, when he was wounded in his left leg.[2] He was taken
to the military hospital at Beelitz, near Berlin, before being transferred to Munich,
two months later, to continue his convalescence.[3] There he wrote to Lanzhammer, a
fellow dispatch-runner in the 16th Bavarian Reserve Infantry Regiment.

As Hitler's words suggest, he was going to return to the front line as soon as he
could, after dental treatment. The postcard, stamped on 19 December 1916, includes
a spelling mistake in the German – *soffort* ('immediately') should just have one 'f'
– perhaps surprising for this later stickler for exactness. According to University of
Aberdeen historian Dr Thomas Weber and author of *Hitler's First War*, the card
offers a rare glimpse of the young Hitler, because once he was in power he diligently
destroyed many documents about his earlier life. Dr Weber said it was also significant
that the future Nazi leader had sent the card to a friend, rather than to his family,
and that he was so eager to return to the front. 'Unlike most other soldiers of Hitler's
regiment who would have been writing home, Hitler didn't stay in touch with his
family during the war, so his regimental headquarters became his surrogate family,'
said Dr Weber. 'Soldiers generally tried to get as much leave as they possibly could to
go back home to see friends and family – it was quite common for a man to overstay
that leave and be willing to suffer the consequences. The contrast here is Hitler; he
doesn't want to be in Munich, he can't wait to get back to the front, and not just the

front, but his particular unit. We know from other sources that in the spring of the following year he was supposed to have been transferred to a different regiment. Instead, Hitler wrote a pleading letter to the commanding officers of his regiment, begging and asking to be transferred back to his regiment and to his old position of dispatch-runner, because that's where his surrogate family is.'

It is possible that Hitler met Lanzhammer – who had served with him at Ypres and on the Somme – in training or by working with him as a dispatch-runner in the 16th Bavarian, which was also known as the 'List Regiment' after its first commander, Colonel Julius von List. Dispatch-runners performed a vital and dangerous role in the days before battlefield radio communication was perfected, conveying orders to the front, and messages back to HQ. However, in Dr Weber's view Hitler's particular job was not quite so courageous. He was tasked with taking messages between regimental headquarters and the HQs of other units, some distance behind the front – a role Dr Weber claims would not have made Hitler popular with his peers in the trenches. The historian says it is also intriguing that Hitler – the future *Führer* of an entire people, and a man who served more than four years at the front

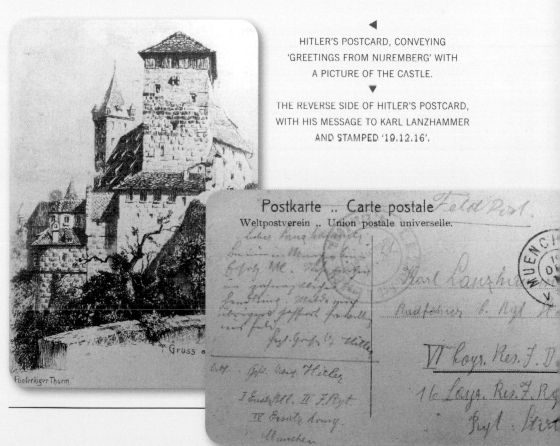

◄

HITLER'S POSTCARD, CONVEYING 'GREETINGS FROM NUREMBERG' WITH A PICTURE OF THE CASTLE.

▼

THE REVERSE SIDE OF HITLER'S POSTCARD, WITH HIS MESSAGE TO KARL LANZHAMMER AND STAMPED '19.12.16'.

and received several awards, including the Iron Cross First Class – never received promotion. 'He remained a normal soldier for the entirety of the war and never had any command over other people,' he said. 'It's been suggested that this was because of class reasons – that his background prevented him becoming an officer – but it could have been that promotion would have meant him leaving the support staff of regimental headquarters, his surrogate family. However, the story is that none of the officers saw any leadership qualities in him. They probably thought he was an excellent soldier in that position – the perfect dispatch-runner – but he was not cut out to lead other people. Strange as it may seem, it was only a year after the war that Hitler underwent a radical transformation in both his political ideals and personality. No-one had seen a future charismatic leader.'

Among those who never witnessed his rise to power was Lanzhammer himself. After serving with Hitler in the 16th Bavarian, he was transferred to the military aviation school in Schleissheim, Bavaria, in September 1917. He was killed in a flying accident during a test flight at Feldmoching on 15 March 1918, aged 21, and is buried in his home town of Dingolfing.

Ian Sayer, a specialist on 20th-century signatures and author of a number of books on Hitler, is certain that the postcard is genuine. Mr Sayer, who has studied Hitler's letters, photographs and documents over 35 years, said: 'I'm quite sure it's Hitler's handwriting. His letters at that particular time aren't rushed and his writing is more legible. His capital letters are almost flowery, relatively flamboyant. Later on, he is a man with a purpose and his writing becomes rushed and business-like, almost like shorthand.'

◄

HITLER (IDENTIFIED BY A CROSS MARKED ON THE PHOTO) WITH THE DISPATCH RUNNERS OF HIS REGIMENT IN THE FRENCH VILLAGE OF FOURNES, TO THE SOUTH OF LILLE, A FEW MILES BEHIND THE FRONT.

The card, which emerged at a family-history roadshow in Munich, was brought in by the son of an anonymous stamp-collector. Frank Drauschke, a historian from the professional research organisation Facts & Files Berlin, researched the provenance of the card and the story associated with it in Germany. 'Hitler was corresponding frequently with Lanzhammer and we were able to trace the card directly to Dingolfing, where Lanzhammer and his family lived,' he said. 'Most probably the card was even presented to the stamp-collector by a family member.' Dr Stuart Lee, of Oxford University, one of the digital experts at the Munich roadshow, said he 'felt a shudder run through me' when he was handed the postcard, which has since been sold at auction. 'While I'm used to handling rare documents, especially medieval manuscripts, this simple card carried an emotional weight that is difficult to describe. Knowing that Hitler had handled it, that this was his handwriting, was an eerie feeling, bearing in mind what we know he then went on to become and the horrors he inflicted on the world.'

Dr Lee's colleague, military historian Dr Stephen Bull said: 'It was a card just like a thousand others we have been offered and photographed for the project; but the one which will most be remembered.' Its significance took a little while to sink in, though. 'When Stuart handed me the card for a first opinion, I was immediately suspicious, since so much Hitler material has been forged or reproduced. However, the materials used, stampings, signature and content soon began to convince. What was particularly interesting, in light of later history, was the choice of Nuremberg for the scene on the obverse.' For it was Nuremburg where the Nazi Party held its mass rallies until 1938, perhaps the most famous of which was the 1934 one, turned by Leni Riefenstahl into the monumental propaganda film *Triumph of the Will*. And it was at Nuremberg where, in 1945–6, leading Nazis were put on trial for their war crimes.

Endnotes

1 The German text reads: *Lieber Lanzhammer / Bin nun in München beim Ersatz Btl. Stehe zur Zeit in zahnärztlicher Be- handlung Melde mich übrigens sofort [sic] freiwillig ins Feld. Hrzl. / Grüsse / A. Hitler*
2 In fact, Hitler was a *Gefreiter*, a rank just above an ordinary private, but not quite a corporal. 'Lance corporal' is therefore an English approximation, though technically a lance corporal is a non-commissioned officer rank, whereas *Gefreiter* was a boosted private.
3 Later Allied propaganda had it that Hitler lost a testicle as a result of his leg injury, and hence the mocking Second World War song: 'Hitler has only got one ball; the other is in the Albert Hall.'

'Big scrap with Huns'
EXPLOITS OF A FLYING ACE

Balancing precariously in an open cockpit at 10,000 feet with nothing but a gun to hold on to, Second Lieutenant Giles Noble Blennerhassett managed to shoot down eight enemy Albatros fighter planes in just three months. He was only 22 when he was awarded the Military Cross for his skill as an aircraft observer in a two-seater F.E.2b, a role that entailed both aerial photography and firing a .303 Lewis light machine gun on a swivel mount from an exposed platform.

Giles was an Irishman, born in Sligo on 16 April 1895. His career in the Royal Flying Corps only began on 24 March 1916, when he was seconded from the 4th

GILES BLENNERHASSETT,
IN UNIFORM.

Battalion, Royal Irish Fusiliers, with whom he had fought in the trenches in France.[1] He was posted to 18 Squadron at the end of 1916, after the squadron had been tasked with flying tactical reconnaissance missions over the trenches of the Somme. Giles's job as an observer-gunner required him to stand in the exposed nose of the plane, clutching his Lewis gun, with the pilot sitting above and behind him. The observer fired forward on a specially designed, swivelling mount that provided a very wide field of fire.

The RFC reconnaissance crews were heroes of the war – bringing vital intelligence about hostile positions and troop movements from high above the battlefield. Their photographic missions helped build up a mosaic map of the enemy trench systems. Pilots and observers were able to direct artillery fire on targets invisible to the gunners on the ground with devastating effect, as well as bomb supply bases. Using the Lewis gun, aircraft became killing machines in their own right, taking part in dogfights with the German Air Service and downing planes with varying degrees of success.

It was this skill of switching between his roles of observer and gunner that secured young Giles Blennerhassett a place in history. During his six weeks of training, which began in January 1917, Giles practised using the Lewis, firing off drums of ammunition and attempting to start the engine. But it was on 4 February

1917 that Giles saw his first piece of action. Manning the guns for fellow ace Robert Farquhar during line patrol duty at 10,000 feet, he drove down a German Albatros D.II north of Le Sars, between Albert and Bapaume. In his log book, he reported: 'Start delayed, engine hard to start. Encountered 4 Huns over NE Le Sars. Shot one down, second one sent down but under control. Had to return with main tank shot through, also radiator.'[2] Giles's flights during the rest of February and March were, however, plagued with problems. He noted on a number of occasions that the mission was curtailed by low cloud cover, writing 'impossible clouds, dense above 4,000 ft', or that his camera had jammed with only 'three photos taken', or that the plane encountered engine trouble – 'engine cut out so returned' or 'returned – engine vibrating'.

But on 5 April 1917, the Irishman's luck changed. On photographic duty with another ace, Victor Huston, he drove down two more D.IIs at Inchy, near Cambrai. '11 photos, but camera dud again. Big scrap with Huns. Got two for certain and another doubtful,' he reported in his log book. On the next day he destroyed another D.II: 'Several Huns about. Had scrap with one over Beugny. Crashed near Beugny.'

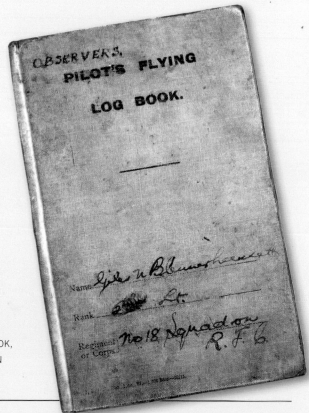

▶

GILES BLENNERHASSETT'S LOG BOOK,
WITH HIS RANK AND SQUADRON
(NO. 18) MARKED IN.

Ten days later, Giles became a *bona fide* flying ace after he downed a fifth D.II –
since airmen gained the coveted 'ace' status after shooting down or destroying five
or more enemy aircraft during combat. He didn't escape entirely Scot free. In his
log book, Giles reported that it had been cloudy when the incident occurred, during
photographic escort duties at 10,000 feet. 'Attacked by 6HA [i.e. six Hun aircraft]
over Cagnicourt. I shot one down and another dropped 2,000 [feet] but recovered
and cleared off. Landed at Beugnatre to have hand dressed.'

Over the next three weeks, Giles was on photographic escort duty almost daily.
On 24 April 1917 he managed to take seven photos until 'Camera jammed. Had to
return. Formation of 20 Huns. Fired two drums. One Hun confirmed.' His entry for
30 April details a 'special mission', which involved dropping 'three bombs on Epinoy.
Fired at 2HA on tail.' Later that day he took part in a night raid: 'Eight bombs at
Epinoy aerodrome. House on fire. Fired drum at train which stopped and sent up
clouds of steam.' The next night he was out again: 'Bombed aerodrome at Eswars.'
During a photographic mission on 3 May, Giles drove down an Albatros D.III into
Bourlon Wood: 'Exposed three plates. Combat 4HA. One sent down vertically.'
[3] Almost three weeks later, on 23 May, he destroyed a D.III and sent another out

AN F.E.2B TWO-SEATER OF THE TYPE THAT GILES BLENNERHASSETT WOULD HAVE
FLOWN IN, SEATED IN THE FRONTAL OBSERVER'S COCKPIT.

of control: 'Combat with 20 HA. One crashed E of Eswars, another on fire.'

After this period of intensive aerial action, on 19 July 1917 Giles was transferred to the RFC Home Establishment, which was responsible for training air and ground crews, preparing squadrons for deployment in France, and providing squadrons for home defence against the German Zeppelin raids. He was awarded the Military Cross a week later, which the *London Gazette* reported was for 'conspicuous gallantry and devotion to duty. He has shown great skill and courage when acting as escort in attacking hostile formations. On one occasion he attacked two hostile machines, driving both out of control. Later, he forced three other machines down.'

In April 1918 the RFC and the Royal Naval Air Service were formed into the new independent air arm, the Royal Air Force. Giles qualified as a pilot, and after the war was appointed as a flying officer, on 24 October 1919. He married and was posted to India, serving with 48 Squadron until October 1920. Giles left the RAF on 22 January 1921, going on to work for a clothing wholesaler in London, and quickly became the company's representative in Ireland. Following his divorce in the mid-1920s, he remarried and he and his second wife set up a business in Dublin, manufacturing knitwear and blouses. Giles Blennerhassett died on 4 December 1978, at the age of eighty-three.

By the end of the First World War, more than 9,000 RFC, RNAS and RAF men had been killed or were missing, and more than 7,000 wounded. It was highly dangerous work. Giles's son Brian, from Dublin, said: 'My father was a very brave man. As an observer he would've been sliding around on a metal floor and having to use the edge of the cockpit to brace himself to fire the weapon. The plane was manoeuvring over the battlefield up to its maximum altitude of 11,000 feet. He would've been thrown all over the place in dog fights with other planes. There were no safety belts or parachutes – how he didn't fall out defies imagination.' [4]

Endnotes

1 The Royal Flying Corps was created in May 1912 to become the British Army's eyes in the sky, and during the First World War its roles included directing artillery gunfire, taking photographs for intelligence analysis, bombing runs, and battling the aircraft of the German Air Service.

2 'Huns' – a derogatory nickname for the Germans used by the British and Americans, harking back to Attila the Hun's Germanic empire in the 5th century.

3 'Exposed three plates' – cameras of the period used glass plate negatives.

4 Brian Blennerhassett provided Giles's log book and a series of photos for this account.

'If you fell off a duckboard you were done for'

A BAPTISM OF MUD

The German machine gun fire from the huge, grey fortress on the outskirts of Ypres was relentless, mowing down great swathes of men as they advanced towards it. Sergeant Charles Carr, among the men of the 2/5 Battalion, Gloucestershire Regiment, continued the charge, despite the fact that many of his friends had fallen around him.[1] It was not long before the 25-year-old sergeant came within the sights of the German machine gunners too, and a couple of bullets hit him in his right thigh, knocking him out of the battle.

CHARLES CARR WITH HIS SISTER EDITH, WHO DIED IN 1916 AGED TWENTY-FIVE.

As his colleagues proceeded onwards, eventually capturing the concrete target, Charles was removed from the battlefield and placed in a shell hole, along with another wounded British soldier and some German POWs. 'My father's friend – Stanley Brunt – went off to get medics for the two of them, but in the meantime, some other stretcher bearers came along and took my father and the other soldier away,' said Charles's son, Tony Carr. 'They hadn't gone more than 100 yards when a shell landed in the hole where they'd just been and everything was blown to smithereens. When Stanley returned with his medics, he assumed my father had died in the blast, so my grandparents had letters and telegrams saying that he was missing believed killed in action – and it was several days before they found out he was just seriously wounded.'

It was on 22 August 1917 that Charles received his wounds during the assault on Pond Farm, a huge emplacement manned by 50 machine-gunners with five guns. Here, the Germans operated out of three large bunkers and a number of small bunkers, tunnels and cellars, with a narrow-gauge railway to the rear providing a supply line to the complex. Until then a number of British divisions had attacked the daunting garrison without success. In addition to the threat of heavy enemy fire across open ground, they had been held back by the atrocious swamp-like conditions that clogged up rifles, made movement difficult, rendered fields impassable and which could suck in horses and even sometimes men. For this was part of the three-month-long Third Battle of Ypres – better known by the name of the village that was its last target, Passchendaele, and the misery of mud, rain and death associated with it.

The offensive was the attempt by the British Army's commander-in-chief Sir Douglas Haig to seize the high ground around Ypres and, if successful, even to sweep through to the Belgian coast and destroy the German submarine bases there. So appalling was the unseasonal rain in August that the attacks were suspended in the

THE TELEGRAM RECEIVED BY CHARLES'S PARENTS, DATED 29 AUGUST 1917,
INFORMING THEM THAT CHARLES WAS 'SERIOUSLY WOUNDED ONLY – NOT DEAD.'

A WAR OFFICE REPORT, DATED 7 SEPTEMBER 1917,
DESCRIBING CHARLES CARR AS BEING ADMITTED TO HOSPITAL
WITH SEVERE GUNSHOT WOUNDS.

first half of the month. Nevertheless, the 2/5th Gloucesters' mission against Pond Farm was successful, albeit costly, claiming the lives of 2 officers and 16 other ranks, wounding 1 officer and 51 other ranks, with another reported as missing – which Charles's family claim was him.

For Charles, the wound to his thigh was his exit out of the trenches. An apprentice draper at 'The Famous of Cheltenham' – an upmarket men's outfitter founded by his uncle Abraham Cole in 1896 – Charles, and his cousins, had been only too willing to join the army when war broke out, even linking arms to march down the town's promenade *en route* to the local recruitment office. [2] Within two years, two of the cousins – Abraham's son Reg and nephew Norman – were killed in action, and Charles was invalided back to Britain with his injured leg. 'The one thing that really struck my father at Passchendaele was the mud,' said Tony Carr who, with his sister Gill Porter, has kept many photos, telegrams and documents relating to his father's First World War service. 'If you fell off a duckboard you were done for. He told me the well known [humorous] story about a chap who stooped down to pick up an Australian hat he'd spotted in the mud and wanted as a souvenir – only to find it was still attached to someone's head. He could see two eyes just peering at him out of the sludge, and as he dragged the man out by his armpits, he turned to him to say: "Steady does it Tommy – I'm on a horse."' Charles's daughter Gill Porter added: 'He also used to tell us how they were plagued by lice and would run a lighted candle up the seams of their uniforms to kill them.'

After he was shot, Charles was taken to an advanced medical station by farm cart, and he was eventually brought back to Southampton 'As all the stretchers were being unloaded on to the quayside, my father said they were met by an elderly woman who came along lighting cigarettes, placing one in each of their mouths,' said Tony. 'It was their first smoke in a long time.' However, as Charles was being admitted to the nearby Royal Victoria Hospital in Netley, his worried parents Caleb Carr (a master draper in Llandrindod Wells, mid-Wales) and his wife Mary Anne Carr (née Cole) were coming to terms with reports that he was missing, believed killed. It was another blow for the couple, who were still reeling from the death of their 23 year old daughter Edith on Christmas Day 1916.

Charles had only found out by chance about Edith when he arrived back on leave in Llandrindod at New Year 1917, to be told by the station master how sorry he was to hear about his sister's death from consumption. 'My father had no idea Edith was even ill,' said Tony. 'So for his parents to be told only a few months later that their only son could also be dead was terribly upsetting for them; it was with great relief they received a postcard from him, and a telegram from his friend Stanley Brunt, saying he was "wounded seriously but going on well".' Another telegram forwarded from Cheltenham said: 'Seriously wounded only, not dead.'

Despite being on home soil, Charles's ordeal was far from over. According to the family, he almost died after dye in his hospital-issue striped pyjamas seeped into his damaged leg. 'The wound was still open and the dye from the pyjamas caused blood poisoning,' said Gill. 'Thankfully he survived, but he always said the dye had caused him more suffering than the wound itself.' Sufficiently recovered, Charles was moved to Seaton Delaval Hall, a country estate near Newcastle, for a period of convalescence. Later he was attached to the 4th Reserve Battalion, Gloucestershire

A WOUNDED CANADIAN SOLDIER IS CARRIED TO A FIRST-AID POST, OCTOBER 1917, AMID THE QUAGMIRE THAT WAS THE BATTLEFIELD OF PASSCHENDAELE.

Regiment, and attended the Northern Command Bombing School in Otley, West Yorkshire, before being posted to Ireland for the rest of the war, to help deal with the continuing unrest in the wake of the 1916 Rising by militant nationalists. He was demobbed on 29 April 1919.

After the Armistice, Charles returned home to Llandrindod, where he joined the family outfitting firm, which he took over upon his father's retirement. 'Before the war, he and his cousin Reg Cole had plans to start their own business together, but those ended when Reg was struck by a bullet in his head at Ploegsteert in May 1915,' said Tony. Charles was in his late thirties when he met his future wife, a young teacher named Evelyn Abery, at a ball in the Metropole Hotel, Llandrindod. 'She and her sister were having car trouble and my father managed to sort it out,' said Tony. 'He followed them back home to make sure they were safe, and when he got there he asked my mother out.' The couple married at St Mary's Church in her home town of Builth Wells, in April 1934, and went on to have their children Tony in 1937 and Gill in 1943.

Charles was almost fifty when the Second World War started, and he served as a sergeant in the Special Constabulary in the old mid-Welsh county of Radnorshire. He died in 1965, aged 73, after he was hit by a car while crossing the road outside his house in Wickhamford, near Evesham, Worcestershire. 'He had only popped out to get something from the village shop,' said Gill. 'My mum heard a screech of brakes, but it was one of the neighbours who ran in and told her what had happened. It was a tragic end for a man who was so full of life. Dad was known for his cheerful personality and would light up any room he entered. He was very proud of being in the First War and regularly attended 2/5th Gloucestershire reunions in Cheltenham. The war had been a tremendous part of his life, but it was something he never dwelt on. I'm sure his good sense of humour and positive nature got him through.'

Endnotes

1 The Gloucestershire Regiment was part of the 184th (2nd South Midland) Brigade.
2 Abraham Cole wrote the poem 'Lest we Forget', which opens: 'Shall we ever forget when the boys marched away, To fight for their King and their home, ...' His shop, The Famous of Cheltenham, closed in 2012 after trading for 116 years.

'A very gallant officer'
AN ORCADIAN AT PASSCHENDAELE

Robert William Taylor was always on a mission to succeed. As a child growing up in the small crofting community of Flotta in the Scottish islands of Orkney, he worked hard at school. He pursued higher education, too, achieving his ambition of a responsible job at the Stromness branch of the National Bank of Scotland. He lost his mother, Jane, aged 44, to meningitis when he was just 7 years old, but Robert – brought up by his father and older sister Mary – was well known for never letting anything stand in the way of what he wanted to do. However, when war broke out in August 1914, and Robert watched many of his friends leave the islands to fight, his plans for a career in the bank changed. Keen not to be left out, he decided work could wait and instead tried to convince his boss that he should be allowed to enlist. Initially, Robert's manager refused to agree; not only was Robert a good worker, whose exam success had secured him admission to the Institute of Bankers in Scotland, he was well liked and had a promising career ahead of him. 'Robert was very clever and had just been promoted, so his manager was loath to see him go,' said

his great-niece Marjorie Manson. 'But he was a headstrong lad who didn't want to be left behind. He didn't want his friends to think he'd been let off the hook – he couldn't bear the shame – so his manager eventually caved in to his pleas and let him go.' Robert enlisted at Kirkwall on 6 July 1915, at the age of 21, and joined the Royal Field Artillery in Glasgow as a gunner.

Robert's ambitious streak stayed with him: he was quickly promoted bombardier, and by 1 October 1915 he

◀

ROBERT TAYLOR, FRESH-FACED AND IN
HIS OFFICER'S UNIFORM.

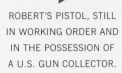
ROBERT'S PISTOL, STILL IN WORKING ORDER AND IN THE POSSESSION OF A U.S. GUN COLLECTOR.

had been recommended for a commission to second lieutenant in the Special Reserve. According to his Active Service Casualty Form he was wounded twice at the Battle of the Somme in September 1916, suffering a small injury on the 12th, which took him out of action for three days, followed by shrapnel wounds to his left arm and shoulder on the 27th, which needed hospital treatment in Boulogne. However, an official telegram sent to his family in Stromness stated it rather more strongly: 'Lieut R.W. Taylor RFA admitted General Hospital, Boulogne, September 29th. Gunshot wounds left arm and right shoulder. Severe.'

He was sent to England for convalescence, and following a short period of leave back in Orkney, in the spring of 1917, he returned to France to take part in the Battle of Arras, a major British-led offensive between April and May that saw the Canadians capture the strategically important Vimy Ridge – but at an ultimate cost of almost 160,000 Allied casualties. Yet Robert managed to escape the battle unscathed, and his division moved on to the Ypres Salient in Belgium, where they were involved in the Third Battle of Ypres – better known by its last phase, the battle for Passchendaele. It opened in mid-July 1917 with 10 days of artillery bombardment of the German lines, consuming more than 4 million shells fired from 3,000 guns. The bombardment destroyed what remained of the drainage system, and together with the relentless unseasonal rain turned the land into a muddy quagmire that made movement difficult and swallowed horses – and sometimes even men. The three-month offensive resulted in almost 600,000 Allied and German casualties. During these attacks, Robert earned a Military Cross for bravery in August. On duty as a Forward Observing Officer, he maintained communications under a heavy barrage; and even after his signallers had become casualties, he directed the fire of his battery's guns to break up two German counter-attacks. The local Orkney newspaper, *The Orcadian*, reported Robert's award, along with news, two weeks later, that he had been promoted lieutenant, adding: 'His many friends in Orkney will be still more pleased to hear of his promotion. All will join in wishing the gallant young officer the very best of luck in his new position.'

Sadly, Robert never lived to receive the prestigious award or enjoy the adulation. He was wounded at Poelcapelle, north-west of Passchendaele, in the final weeks of the battle, and he died – aged 24 – at the 47th Casualty Clearing Station on 24 October 1917. Robert's father received a telegram informing him of his son's death two days later. Again, *The Orcadian* reported on Robert's fate, noting: 'Lieutenant Taylor was not only a very gallant officer, but an excellent young man, of a disposition that made everyone who knew him his friend.' Robert's great-niece Marjorie said that his sister Mary never got over his death. 'Mary had taken it upon herself to bring Robert up after their mother died when he was little – so to lose him so suddenly was devastating. She was in mourning for the rest of her life and never wore anything other than black.'

Robert's MC was sent to his father in Flotta in March 1918, but the family were so upset they decided against applying for his War Medal and Victory Medal. Instead, they put up a large photo of the fresh-faced uniformed young officer in the parlour of the family home as a constant reminder of his bravery and of what they had lost. However, during a clear-out of the house in the 1990s by one of Robert's nephews, the picture was discarded. Marjorie said that her mother, Clara Sutherland, thought she would never see it again, until it was rescued from a skip by a council worker in Shetland, who thought it was too precious an item to throw away. 'Luckily, the picture was returned to Orkney and appeared in *The Orcadian*,' said Marjorie. 'My mother – who was Robert's niece – saw the picture and said: "That's my Uncle Robbie." She donated the photo and Military Cross to Orkney Museum in Kirkwall, along with Robert's compass in 2002.'

In a strange turn of events, Robert's story went overseas in 2008, when what is believed to be his pistol, a Webley Mk V service revolver, was put up for sale on an online auction site that specialises in guns. Military weapons' collector Alan Casida, from Kansas, who owns 40 firearms – including nine from the First World War – bought it for $650 (£425). 'It still gives me a little chill when I pick it up,' he said. 'It is in good condition and has "R.W. Taylor RFA" clearly stamped on the back strap. There are little splatter marks here and there on the gun where the finish is gone. While I cannot say what took the finish off, I do know that blood will remove the bluing from a gun. I have shot the revolver and that in itself was quite a sobering experience. Many thoughts went through my head about him carrying it on the battlefield and the likelihood of it being on his person when he was killed. Even though it is my most prized gun in my collection, nothing would make me happier than if I could somehow return it to Orkney where it might be displayed in the Kirkwall museum with Lt Taylor's other personal items.'

Robert is buried at Dozinghem Military Cemetery, Poperinge (Poperinghe), in West Flanders, and is commemorated on Stromness and Flotta war memorials, as well as inside Flotta church near his family home. Marjorie visited her great-uncle's grave at Dozinghem in November 2008, fulfilling a promise that she had made to herself following her mother's death four years earlier. 'My mum was very proud of her uncle, so I wanted to see his grave just for her,' she said. 'Reading the inscription that says he was a native of Flotta was very emotional. Robert was such a brave man who knew what he wanted and was never afraid to go out and get it. Unfortunately, as for many Orcadians during the First World War, that courage cost him his life.'

THE TELEGRAM INFORMING ROBERT'S FAMILY THAT HE HAD SUFFERED SEVERE GUNSHOT WOUNDS TO HIS LEFT ARM AND RIGHT SHOULDER.

'They were inseparable'
REVOLUTION, MARRIAGE AND
A TALE OF TWO WARS

As blacksmith Mihael Drašček toiled away in his workshops at Ozeljan, a small village not far from Gorizia (Gorica), church bells rang out to announce the onset of war in 1914. The peals, which echoed across Slovenia's Lower Vipava valley – then still part of the Austro-Hungarian Empire – marked the start of a new life for the blond-haired, blue-eyed 25 year old. Within days of the outbreak of war, Mihael had joined the army – more specifically, the 7th Company, KK 'Imperial and Royal' Austro Hungarian *Landwehr* Mountain Regiment No. 4 – and was fighting the Russians on the Eastern Front, in Galicia. During a series of battles that saw the Russians force the Austro-Hungarian armies back to the Carpathian Mountains, Mihael suffered a leg wound and was taken prisoner. He was sent to Tashkent, then capital of Russian Turkistan (now in Uzbekistan).

It was during his captivity that Mihael's progressive views were reignited. As a

MIHAEL DRAŠČEK (*CENTRE, WITH GUITAR*) AND COMPANIONS IN RUSSIAN CAPTIVITY.

young man, he had been an active member in the Sokol Society and head of its local section. The Sokol ideology promoted national and cultural awareness through physical education. Many Slovenes resented Austro-Hungarian rule and, according to the Sokol movement, a nation's aspirations to be truly democratic and free also meant that its people had to be physically fit and morally strong. It was a code that Mihael followed to the letter. His family said he was a typical Sokol disciple – a strong, active man, who loved cycling and never stood still. He was also an idealist, who believed in Slovenian independence. As a POW, Mihael continued to work as a blacksmith, but he was also able to observe the growing political unrest in Russia. He used his time to study the revolutionary Marxist ideals of the Bolsheviks and, finding himself sympathetic to their cause,

THE ARISTOCRATIC JANINA ELIZABETA MAZURKIEWICZ, WHO LEFT BEHIND A PRIVILEGED LIFE TO DEVOTE HERSELF TO MIHAEL.

Mihael took part in the revolutionary movement, even fighting with their troops during the Bolsheviks' seizure of power: the October Revolution of 1917.[1]

While it is not known if Mihael actually joined the Bolshevik Party, his links with the movement came to an abrupt end after he was captured by Mensheviks, the less hardline Marxists who had split from the Bolsheviks over a decade before and were vying with them for power. Mihael was again in prison. But there his plight came to the attention of Janina Elizabeta Mazurkiewicz, a Polish woman of noble decent, who secured his release in a most unusual way. Janina, from Lublin – at that time under Austro-Hungarian control, as part of Galicia – had fled to Moscow on the outbreak of war, and then on to the central regions of Russia's empire. The family believe that she met and fell in love with Mihael after meeting him in a pub that POWs were able to use – and then told the Menshevik prison authorities that the pair were due to marry, pleading with them to let him go. Believing her story, they set Mihael free, and the couple duly wed a short while later. 'From that day forward they were inseparable,' said their grand-daughter Rada Čopi. 'It's possible she was attracted by his enthusiasm or liveliness. He was, after all, always the centre of attention – a very active, brave, vivacious and sociable person; a diligent organiser, always striving for the common good. But Janina was very, very attached to him, and without him, she refused to do anything.'

The couple had initially planned to settle back in Lublin, soon after the war, but the severe winter and an impassable route made that impossible. Instead, they moved first to Hammerstein, near Bonn, in Germany, where they had a little girl, Marija, and then on to Berlin. Years later, the family decided to return to Mihael's home village of Ozeljan, but chaotic postwar circumstances and new borders complicated their journey. By now, Ozeljan had become Italian territory. They were detained in the northern Slovenian town of Jesenice for some weeks, before they could travel to Ozeljan, where Mihael took over his family's blacksmith business. After the birth of their sons – Janko and Stanko – Janina became a major part of the village community. She opened a small tobacco shop and learned Slovenian, although she never lost her Polish accent.

However, family life came to an abrupt end during the Second World War. Their son Stanko fled the village to join the Slovenian partisans, who were fighting against the German and Italian occupiers, and was killed during a visit to see his parents. 'He was just leaving their house when he saw an armoured vehicle and began to run,' said Rada. 'Because his actions looked suspicious, he was shot by collaborators. When they discovered he was armed, they gathered all the villagers together to ask if anyone recognised his dead body. Janina and Miha were so scared that if they said he was their son the lives of other villagers would be in danger, they claimed they did not know him.' Stanko had been a lively 19 year old, and his death affected his parents greatly. 'They were left in shock and would not speak about what happened for many years,' said Rada.

◄

MIHAEL'S WOODEN CHEST
WHICH TRAVELLED WITH HIM
EVERYWHERE, THROUGH THE WAR
AND RUSSIAN REVOLUTION, AND
BACK HOME TO SLOVENIA.

After the Second World War, Mihael tried to improve the lives of his fellow villagers. He oversaw the construction of a freshwater supply to Ozeljan and encouraged locals to get more involved in the community. 'Strangely, my grandfather lived in three different countries during his lifetime, even though he only left his native home occasionally,' said Rada. 'He was born in the Austro-Hungarian monarchy and was mobilised as its soldier. When he returned home from Russian captivity, his village became part of Italy; but after the Second World War it belonged to the former Yugoslavia. Following his death and Slovenia's independence in 1991, the village became part of the Republic of Slovenia.'

In their later years, the couple lived with their son Janko and his family, until Janina died in 1967, and Mihael ten years later. 'Miha never forgot what Janina had given up to be with him,' said Rada, the eldest of Janko's three children. [2] 'As a landowner's daughter, she had enjoyed quite a privileged lifestyle. Miha did what he could to help her adjust – even building her an improvised bathroom with a big mirror so she didn't have to use the public tap in the middle of the village. Unlike her female neighbours, Janina was not a very skilled housewife and gardener and had been quite surprised that she would not have a cook when they moved to Ozeljan. But the two of them were completely devoted to each other. Even in old age, they talked late into the night about past events and people they had met before they returned to Miha's home. They had so much fun, roaring across the country on their motorbike visiting friends. I'll never forget Janina's long dark hair which she braided into a fishtail, or how much time she'd spend looking for her lost monocle. To her, Miha was the love of her life. She'd tell anyone who would listen how brave and fearless he was, yet tell him, with the biggest smile: "You are my rascal, my big rascal!"'

Endnotes

1 In the Western calendar, the revolution actually happened in November 1917. Lenin's Bolsheviks toppled Russia's Provisional Government, which had been attempting to run the country – and its fading war effort – after the Tsar had abdicated in February 1917, but in the face of continuing economic crisis, shortages, army mutinies, civil unrest and political threats from Right and Left. The Bolshevik coup in the capital, Petrograd (St Petersburg), was speedy and almost without violence; other major cities fell throughout Russia to Bolshevik control too, with varying levels of opposition, as Lenin proclaimed a new era of government by 'soviets' (councils).

2 Apart from hearing the story first-hand from her grandparents, Rada Čopi was able to produce passports, postcards and other documents about their lives from Mihael Drašček's heavy wooden trunk, which travelled everywhere with him.

'It was a miracle'
YOU ONLY LIVE TWICE

The German attack on the trench where Belgian bugler Achille Amand Duprez and his colleagues had taken cover came quickly and by surprise. No sooner had troops from the Belgian 3rd Rifle Brigade (3ième Régiment Chasseurs à Pied) been sent to an advanced position, less than half a mile from the River Yser, than they were overwhelmed by an enemy sortie crossing the water, brandishing rifles and bayonets. As the attackers came closer, the Flemish-speaking infantrymen faced an even more fearsome weapon – the flamethrower. 'The fight was terrible', according to Dagobert Duprez-Delbaere, Achille's nephew. 'Within moments, the Germans succeeded in burning out the whole trench. All that was left were charred bodies – none of the victims were recognisable. My uncle had been among the group, but all that was left of him was his bugle. Naturally, his unit assumed he was among the dead and they were buried in a military cemetery at Oeren, near Dixmude.'

The attack had taken place on 18 March 1918, just three days before the start of the German Spring Offensive – Germany's last great push to win the war. By then Achille had been on the Western Front for four years, serving in the 3rd Army Division along the Belgian lines in Ramskapelle (near Nieuwpoort), Pervijze (Pervyse) and Oud-Stuivekenskerke (north of Dixmude). News that he had been killed was a devastating blow for his parents, Cyriel and Leonie Slosse, who had believed that Achille – the third of their four sons – was going places. The couple, who owned a bakery and grocer's shop in Bellegem, West Flanders, had sent him after his primary school education to Pecq, near the border with France. There they hoped he might improve his French and thus further his career prospects. 'They believed having a working knowledge of French was indispensable for the "Flemish yokel" if he wanted a little respect and to achieve something in Belgium,' said Dagobert. When the war broke out, Achille was 21 and working as a clerk at the railway station in nearby Kortrijk (Courtrai); but, eager to serve his country, he joined the 3rd Rifle Brigade as a bugler, with the job of sounding calls to relay orders to his comrades.

▶

ACHILLE DUPREZ, THE SOLDIER WHO 'DIED TWICE',
STANDING NEXT TO HIS OWN GRAVE.

For nine months after March 1918, Achille's family mourned his death, paying regular visits to his grave; so it came as a shock when, in December 1918, he arrived back at the family home in Bellegem. 'My grandparents couldn't believe their eyes,' said Dagobert. 'It was like having someone back from the dead – it was a miracle. So much time had passed, so many things had happened. They had mourned his death and were beginning to move on – and then he arrives back alive and well. He told them that when the Germans had attacked his trench with their flamethrowers, instinctively he had jumped out. He was stabbed by a German bayonet which cost him one of his lungs. He was taken across the river as a prisoner of war and treated in a hospital in Ghent.' A month after he was injured, Achille was transferred to the *Kriegsgefangenenlazarett*, or hospital for POWs, in the central German town of Ohrdruf, south of Gotha, Thüringen. By September, he was moved to the Camp Langensalza, north of Gotha, and then to Camp Göttingen, Hanover, before he was repatriated on 7 December 1918.[1] 'When my uncle came home he donned his army attire and had a photograph taken next to his own grave,' said Dagobert. 'He had the picture framed and it stayed on the wall of his office for many years. Unfortunately, his family were more interested in the frame than the photo and it could easily have disappeared, so now it has come to me.'

GERMAN INFANTRYMEN TRAIN WITH A FLAMETHROWER,
THE FEARED WEAPON THAT ALMOST INCINERATED ACHILLE DUPREZ.

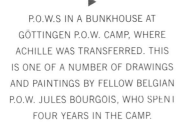

P.O.W.S IN A BUNKHOUSE AT GÖTTINGEN P.O.W. CAMP, WHERE ACHILLE WAS TRANSFERRED. THIS IS ONE OF A NUMBER OF DRAWINGS AND PAINTINGS BY FELLOW BELGIAN P.O.W. JULES BOURGOIS, WHO SPENT FOUR YEARS IN THE CAMP.

After the war, Achille returned to work at the railway station in Kortijk, but he continued to feel aggrieved that the Flemish working-class boys he fought alongside had been addressed by officers in French – a language they hardly understood. He became a Flemish radical and president of the Bellegem VOS – Flemish Old Warriors – the pacifist and nationalist organisation. 'Each year he took part in the pilgrimage to the Yser Tower – the location where he escaped death, but lost a lot of pals,' said Dagobert. [2] Achille Duprez died – for real – in Bissegem, on 19 December 1964. Dagobert felt that Achille had always 'found it difficult to talk about what had happened to him – he always had to be prompted. After all, it is quite an unbelievable story – there can't be many people who die twice and are buried twice – but my uncle was, and I have the photo to prove it.'

Endnotes

1 The family memories are backed up by Achille's military file, which also shows he was decorated for his war service (Victory Medal, Memorial Medal, War Cross and Fire Cross, awarded to those under fire at the front).

2 'Yser Tower' – a memorial built by veterans (*see* Endnote 3, page 79).

'What better epitaph?'
ACTS OF KINDNESS AND SALVATION

On the day James Burke left his home in Dublin to join the British Army, in 1915, his mother placed a crucifix in his left breast pocket. It was a maternal act of kindness for which he would be eternally grateful.

James was the third child of Jane and Edmund Burke, born in Dublin's Charlemont Street in 1895. He had an elementary education and was working at the Princess Cinema, in the city's Rathmines area, when war broke out in 1914. At the age of 19 he joined the 1st Battalion, Royal Irish Fusiliers, whose unofficial motto was 'Faugh-a-Ballagh' (Clear the Way). He was well regarded by the cinema's managing director J.J. Bradlaw, who wrote in a farewell character reference (21 July 1915): 'Mr James Burke has been in our employ for the past two years; during which time we have always found him strictly honest, sober, willing and obliging, tidy and clean, and leaves at his own request to join the Colours. His position will be always open when he is discharged. All wages paid up to date and cards stamped.'

In an interview almost 90 years later, James's son Gary said his father had decided to enlist so he would not be a burden to his family. James's father had died of complications from a dog bite, shortly after James was born, and in 1899 James's mother remarried – a farrier called John Lawless. Two years later, James acquired a step-brother, John. By 1911, there were eight people living at the family home in St James's Street, Dublin, including the couple, their four children and two lodgers – a tailor and a cook/domestic servant. But James's decision to help out financially was probably not his only motive for joining the British Army. Many in Ireland – which was still entirely within the United Kingdom – supported the war effort across the political spectrum, from the pro-British Unionists to mainstream nationalists.[1] Conscription was never introduced in Ireland, even after its general introduction on the British mainland in 1916; but approximately 200,000 Irishmen volunteered to serve in the British forces, and about 30,000 of them died. So adventure, duty and patriotism also played their part in spurring men to enlist, especially early on.

The 1st Battalion, Royal Irish Fusiliers, fought on the Western Front for most of the war, becoming part of the 36th (Ulster) Division in August 1917. By the spring of 1918, British intelligence was anticipating a major German offensive, and on 21 March it duly began with unprecedentedly intense, though brief, artillery bombardments against the Allies, gas attacks, and 'infiltration' by German stormtroopers. These lightly equipped troops flowed around the British positions, disrupting communications and leaving isolated pockets of defenders to be mopped up later. Launched by General Erich Ludendorff, the German Spring Offensive was an attempt to defeat the Allies before the arrival of substantial numbers of American troops, and so bring the war on the Western Front to a swift conclusion. When the onslaught commenced on 21 March, James was – according to son Gary – guarding a bridge near St Quentin with five other soldiers when a German sniper trained a rifle on his chest. The shot that was fired ricocheted off the left arm of the crucifix, still in his breast pocket, away from his heart and into his shoulder. He fell into a frozen trench, and, according to his family, he lay there for up to three days.

James's nephew Desmond Lawless said: 'He was found by a German officer who took him over to their medical staff to treat him. The ground was so cold, the blood in the wound froze over, otherwise he would have bled to death. My Uncle Jimmy said he was exceptionally well treated by the German medical people and when he was more or less fully recovered, he was made a Prisoner of War.' Gary added, in an interview recorded in 2002: 'Not only did he get a serious wound from a bullet, but he went through life with no toe nails from the cold, and a bad chest from mustard gas. The Germans shot my father. A German officer saved my father's life and a German surgeon operated to save his life. For the rest of his life my father would never let anyone say a bad word about a German and he had the right. They tried to kill him and they saved him; so what better epitaph?'

▶

JAMES BURKE'S LIFE-SAVING CRUCIFIX,
GIVEN TO HIM BY HIS MOTHER.

THE BRITISH RED CROSS POSTCARD ENQUIRING ABOUT PRIVATE JAMES BURKE, PRESUMED MISSING ON 21 MARCH 1918 – FIRST DAY OF THE GERMAN SPRING OFFENSIVE.

Desmond Lawless says he believes that his uncle, being a POW, was sent to work in a salt mine in Poland. However, the first James's mother heard about her son's predicament was when she received a German postcard addressed to 'MRS J. LAWLESS / 7 Fennells Cottage / off Charlemont Street / Dublin, IRELAND', which was postmarked 'Stendal'(about 80 miles west of Berlin), and which bore the date 7 June 1918 and the pre-printed declaration: 'I am prisoner of war in Germany'. According to his family, the card, which confirmed that he was wounded, bore James's handwriting; but his writing was shaky and unsteady. [2]

The end of the war brought repatriation for James. According to Gary, his father returned home a religious man with a particular devotion to the French St Thérèse of Lisieux, also known as St Thérèse, 'The Little Flower'. He took up his career at the cinema again, and when he learnt that the young woman working in a confectionary shop across the road was called Teresa, he took it as a sign. He married Teresa O'Connor in the late 1920s and they went to live in her family home in Dublin, where they had the basement as a living room and kitchen space, and a bedroom on the second floor. Their daughter Ethna was born on 22 April 1929, followed by Gary on 14 July 1937. Gary, who died on 7 March 2003, said he remembered as a child being fascinated by his father's war wound. 'When da used to be having a bath, I'd be pushing my fingers into both ends of his wound wondering if I pushed hard enough would they meet,' he said.

Desmond Lawless said his Uncle Jimmy was like a father figure to him. 'When my dad lost his job as an electrician early on in the Second World War he had to go to Belfast to work in the shipyards. Every time I got into bother with my bike, my Uncle Jimmy was always available to do repairs on it. He more or less took the place of my father when he was in the shipyards. He worked at the Theatre Deluxe in Camden Street, Dublin, and he was always impeccably dressed. His shoes were highly polished and he always had a clean collar and tie. I put this down to the fact he had been in the British Army.'

James Burke was still a cinema worker when he died on 22 January 1953, aged 57; but the act of humanity shown by the German officer who saved him from certain death in 1918 lives on. The story, told many times by Gary to Don Mullan, the husband of his god-daughter Margaret, sparked the Christmas Truce Project, which aims to create a Flanders Peace Field at Messines, in memory of the Christmas Truce of 1914 when both sides laid down their arms to exchange food, swap cap badges and share photographs. Gary entrusted Don, the project's ambassador, with James's memorabilia, which included the bullet-marked crucifix, James's service medals and two small German medals, which he equally treasured – perhaps as a reminder of the young officer who saved his life. 'To me the story of the German soldier being moved with compassion to help the wounded James Burke is another example of humanity in the midst of the carnage of the First World War,' said Don. 'It is, in a sense, the Christmas Truce in miniature. It allows us to recognise that no one, including nations, is ever entirely bad.'

Endnotes

1 Exceptions to this consensus were the more militant nationalists of, for example, the Irish Republican Brotherhood and Irish Volunteers, who mounted the challenge to British rule in the Easter Rising of 1916. Their support grew thereafter, but in 1914 radical nationalists were in the minority.
2 James's son Gary also kept a postcard from the British Red Cross and Order of St John and addressed to the Enquiry Department for Wounded and Missing, dated 15 July 1918, which stated that Private James Burke, Regiment No. 20864 of the Royal Irish Fusiliers 1st Battalion, went missing on 21 March 1918. A further document relating to James, stamped 'REPATRIATED PRISONER OF WAR', had the handwritten date of 5 January 1919.

'The pair fell in love'
A TRANSATLANTIC TRYST

Marguerite Bourguignon always made a point of being different and had a way with her that constantly attracted attention. As a child growing up in Langres, in north-eastern France, she lived in a beautiful mansion provided for the family by the French army, where her father Jean was a lieutenant. Regular parties in the park afforded her the opportunity to dress up in silk crinoline dresses and voluminous hats; she claimed she was only ever upstaged by her mother, Marie, who would arrive at any event as though she was on her way to a ball. For Marguerite, who was born in the town in 1895, life was easy and fun. However, shortly after her grandfather Nicholas Bourguignon – Jean's father – died in 1904, the good times came to an end. Within three years it became obvious that Jean's brother and mother could not cope with running the family farm, winery and wooden shoe-making business, so it was decided that Jean, Marie, Marguerite and her older brother Albert would take over. Thus, the family moved from Langres to Nicholas's house in nearby Esnoms-au-Val, a place where life could not have been quieter, compared to the city life to which they had become accustomed.

Unlike his father, Jean Bourguignon had never wanted to be a farmer; instead he had broken away to attend a military school, and he joined the army as soon as he could. His father's death had brought him right back to where he started. Now, rather than enjoying the off-duty social scene in Langres at weekends, his time at home often involved having to help bring in the grape harvest. The move to such a small rural village also came as a complete shock to Marguerite, who was by then aged twelve. Her great-niece Francine Fuqua said: 'She was stunned when she discovered there was no running water or electricity, that no-one ever dressed up except for their trip to church, that there were always cows, horses and chickens crossing the streets and the village had only 275 inhabitants, most of whom she viewed as "uneducated farmers". She resented having to help with family tasks; after all, neither she nor her mother was particularly suited to farming life. Her mother's elegant clothes and her father's visits in his officer's uniform only reinforced the opinion locally that these were "upper-class folks". Marguerite also made a point of being "different" and was considered by villagers as a bit of a "character" – something she enjoyed playing to

MARGUERITE BOURGUIGNON WITH HER PET GOAT TITINNE,
WHOSE HOOVES SHE PAINTED GOLD. SHE TRADED RUSTIC FRENCH LIFE
FOR MARRIAGE AND THE NEW WORLD.

the max. She told me she would put on an organza dress and high heels to walk her pet goat Titinne through the village, even though the streets were uneven, covered in hay and animal excrement. She painted Titinne's hooves gold and placed a ribbon and a bell around her neck – she said the pair of them looked quite a sight.'

However, by 1913 the family suffered another blow. Jean, who had risen through the army ranks to captain, suffered a kidney infection and died, aged 54, leaving Marguerite's mother Marie on her own to take care of the farming business. For Marguerite, who was by then 18, her father's death meant she had to take on even more chores. Her brother Albert had left to study at the prestigious military academy at St Cyr, so it was down to Marguerite to help tin the cherries, peaches, apples and pears from their enormous orchards; gather eggs and churn butter; and distribute fresh vegetables and a freshly slaughtered chicken to the church every other day for the poor, something her deeply religious mother took great pride in.

By the time war broke out in 1914, Albert had graduated from St Cyr – along with the future President of the French Fifth Republic, Charles de Gaulle – and went on to become one of the first few pilots of the French Air Force. The income from the farm was dwindling, and with the departure of all the men to war, life for Marguerite appeared bleak. 'She said the years from 1913 to 1917 were the worst in her life,' remembered Francine. However, in 1917 everything changed. The United States joined the war and the American Expeditionary Force began to arrive in many French towns and villages. Esnoms' proximity to the heavily fortified city of Langres made it an attractive prospect for billeting officers and their men, and Marguerite said her mother was hugely relieved when she was asked to rent out accommodation to various US units. During the war years, many American servicemen stayed on the vast farm, including the 315th Infantry, the 114th Infantry, the 326th Infantry and the US Army Corps of Engineers.[1] While the officers stayed in the main residence, the other ranks bunked in barns. Some stayed a matter of days, while others lived there for months. 'Marguerite and her mother's lives changed overnight,' said Francine. 'Busy with young men coming in eager to taste her great cooking, Marie prepared many meals for them, although the army did provide rations and canned goods. She often helped them to wash their clothes and Marguerite would hang them in the backyard to dry. After supper, Marguerite would go in to the orchard behind the house and, with the help of a dictionary, she tried to learn about the soldiers' homes in America. She told me that most of the men she met came from the northern US – New York, Pennsylvania, New Jersey, Delaware and a few from California.'

According to Francine, Marguerite welcomed the attention of the American soldiers, particularly since so many of the eligible Frenchmen had left the area to go to war. 'She told me there was a very handsome American with whom she began a special relationship, but her mother put an end to it immediately,' said Francine. However, as the months went by Marie gave up trying to keep her beautiful daughter away from the US servicemen. Despite her initial reservations, she also became quite fond of the men who stayed in her home and described them as 'my Yanks', whose company she enjoyed 'even though they chewed on that horrible gum incessantly and put their feet on the table,' she would often say. 'Marguerite said her

THOMAS ('TIMMY') MONCURE IN UNIFORM, DURING THE WAR. UNKNOWN TO MARGUERITE, HE WAS MARRIED AT THE TIME.

mother admired their positive attitude in the midst of such a horrible war,' said Francine. 'They often came to supper covered in mud, exhausted from their work with their units during the day, but they were still smiling and upbeat.'

By 1918, Marguerite was 23 and she told Francine she would often walk through the village with her new US friends, smoking a cigar, just to raise eyebrows. She encouraged one of the villagers to teach the Americans *pétanque* in front of her farm, and even joined in – then a rare event for a woman. [2] However, Marguerite's eyes were soon focused on just one of the guests at the farm – Thomas Moncure, a lieutenant from the 29th Engineers, whose US Army printing press at Langres produced millions of maps for the war effort. The unit was also tasked with securing information on enemy activities, locating batteries and general observation. 'Despite the 13-year age difference, the pair fell in love immediately,' said Francine.

Towards the end of the war many Americans went home, but Thomas, whom Marguerite called 'Timmy', remained for a short while to hear and record local claims for damages incurred during the eight-month stay of the 29th Engineers. [3] 'When it was his time to leave, Timmy promised to return to France to marry Marguerite as soon as possible,' said Francine. 'She went to Paris in 1919 to choose her wedding

MARGUERITE, THE AMERICAN, AT HER LATER HOME IN LOS ANGELES.

gown, veil and shoes; she waited and waited and kept corresponding with him, but still he did not come. She was despondent and very angry. Finally, in late 1922, he told her that all that time he was married and trying to get a divorce. She was astonished – he had never mentioned having a wife in the US. Finally, on June 16, 1923 they married in Paris and they left for a new life in America just days later.'

According to the family, the couple moved to Glendale, California, where Timmy was employed to help survey and plan the Los Angeles road layout. 'Marguerite returned to France in the late 1920s and arrived in Esnoms dressed in the latest fashions of the time, with her hair cut into a neat bob and smoking a long elegant cigar – needless to say she once again astonished the villagers,' said Francine, who also lives in the United States, in Tennessee. 'She almost died laughing as she recalled trying to teach the Charleston to some of her girlhood friends in the village square, with many of them wearing heavy wooden clogs.' Her mother Marie did visit her once in 1930, two years before she died, and spent much of the trip marvelling at how many denominations of church there were – and how the bars and taverns almost outnumbered them, despite Prohibition. Marguerite and Timmy never had children, but even in her dotage she still lived up to her reputation as a character. 'When she was almost 80 years old I would visit her in the courtyard of her home, a long cigar in her mouth, dressed in her nightgown, long grey hair flowing in the breeze, feeding hundreds of birds,' said Francine. 'Marguerite died in her sleep aged

94 in 1989 and is buried next to her beloved Timmy in Forest Lawn, the prestigious cemetery in Glendale that is used as a resting place by many Hollywood celebrities, including Elizabeth Taylor and Clark Gable.'

After the loss of such a big personality, Marguerite's family came across one final memory of the US soldiers who had changed her life. 'My cousin Patrick Flocard, who lives in the Esnoms home, was moving bales of hay in order to repaint the barn when he discovered mementoes inscribed on the walls by three American soldiers who had stayed there in 1918,' said Francine. 'He also found a blackened piece of chewing gum stuck on the same wall, still with the imprint of a finger pushing against it – I'm sure my great-grandmother would not have liked that.' One of the messages says: *'Vive le Amerique and Vive la France,* from JP Barinque 326 Inf, Nov 17, 1918', while 'Edw Clark' of the '114th US Inf' says simply: 'Now in Berlin'. 'Charles Fenstermacher of the 315 Inf Band' just added the date of his stay, 'July 25 – Sep 8, 1918'. 'So far I have found out that Barinque was originally of French descent, was wounded during the war and received the Purple Heart,' said Francine.[4] 'Fenstermacher lived in Schuylkill Haven, Pennsylvania, and became a tin smith and played the clarinet. The one person I've been unable to trace is Edw Clark, who put that he was based at Camp McClellan, Anniston, Alabama. I would dearly love to solve that mystery; if nothing else to keep the story of my great-aunt's wartime adventures going for a bit longer.'

Endnotes

1 The varied roles of the US Army Corps of Engineers in France included repairing bridges and roads, maintaining communication lines, removing land mines, digging trenches, constructing buildings such as hospitals and barracks, and providing clean water.
2 *'Pétanque'* – the game played on gravel, which involves throwing hollow metal balls as close as possible to a small wooden ball called a *cochonnet*.
3 According to Richard T. Evans and Helen M. Frye, *History of the Topographical Branch (Division)*, no date, p. 79: 'Prior to Armistice Day, when the orders came in June (1918) to return, the 29th Engineers marched out of the Tureen Barracks with flags flying and its fine band playing, paraded through the main street of Langres and down the winding road to the railroad, and entrained for the ports of St. Nazaire and Brest. Only one American remained in Langres: Lt. Thomas H. Moncure, who was to hear and record claims for damages incurred by the French townspeople during the 8-months stay of the 29th Engineers in Langres. (December 3, 1917 to June 20, 1918).'
4 'Purple Heart' – awarded in the name of the US president to soldiers wounded or killed while serving under the US military on or after 5 April 1917.

'It was absolutely concentrated hell'
A PRISONER'S DIARY

As his men awoke to a terrific barrage of enemy fire, Second Lieutenant Ronald Alexander Macdonald was forced to give them a very quick lesson on how to fight back. The 174th company of the Royal Engineers – a tunnelling unit largely made up of experienced coal miners – was more used to packing explosives under enemy trenches or digging machine-gun positions than using weapons in anger. But on 21 March 1918, Ronald's sappers found themselves caught up in the start of the German Spring Offensive, which opened with a million artillery shells being fired at British lines in northern France in just five hours, and more than 20,000 British soldiers being taken prisoner by nightfall.

Among the captives was 21-year-old Ronald, a mining engineer who had trained as an officer in Glasgow and was just 18 when war broke out. Born in South Africa, he was orphaned while he was fighting in France, leaving his little sister Mary, who was eight years his junior, in the care of their Aunt Meg. Throughout his four years at the front, Ronald's almost fatherly concern for his sister's wellbeing is evident in his letters back home; but while he touched on his capture in many missives to her, he reserved the full horror of the events before and afterwards for his war diary.

His account relates how the 21 March attack on his men began at 5am, with their dugout receiving a direct hit, gas being detected and the arrival of a stream of wounded soldiers. The bombardment forced Ronald and his captain, Peter Whitehead, to order their sappers to take up arms and man a sunken road near Noreuil. 'It was a miracle none of us was hit as shells were bursting all round us,' recorded Ronald. 'I mounted the bank of the road to see how matters stood and saw the Bosche arriving over in thousands, line after line.' As the attack continued, Ronald was hit by pieces of shell, which bruised his hip. Captain Whitehead was not so lucky. 'Poor old Whitey got killed in going over – he was shot through the head and died instantaneously. He was a topping chap – one of the best,' said Ronald.

Ronald's sappers moved on and took shelter in a half-dug trench along with some infantry, but they were far from safe. 'The enemy soon appeared and we came under machine-gun fire from both sides of the trench,' he wrote. 'Sapper Nuttis got shot through the face at my side as I was pointing out some Bosche to him. As he fell with the blood gushing from his face and mouth, he gasped out: "Sir!" I explained to my sappers how to use the Mills Bomb [grenade]. They never had had any military training and some of the poor old lads didn't even know how to shoot right. Getting hold of a rifle, I lay behind the parapet and had some shots at a Bosche. He disappeared. I hope I got him. I was pointing out Jerries on the other side of us to Sapper Davidson; he was just going to fire when some dirt spurted up in our faces and the poor old lad fell dead with a dull "Oh!" He was shot through the head. It was just a matter of inches in both cases.' As the machine-gun bombardment became more intense, an enemy aeroplane flew over, firing into Ronald's trench and forcing him to withdraw his men to the sunken road, where he spotted two infantrymen. 'As they did not seem to know what to do, and our position in the sunken road was critical, I got what sappers I had, ran across the road and got into a trench which ran

RONALD MACDONALD (*BACK ROW, THIRD FROM LEFT*) WITH HIS FELLOW OFFICERS.

RONALD'S DIARY ENTRY, INCLUDING MAP OF THE GERMAN ATTACK,
FOR 21 MARCH 1918, THE DAY OF HIS CAPTURE.

back. The infantry followed. Somehow or other we got word that reinforcements were coming up, so we manned the trench on both sides as the enemy were working down on us from both flanks. Soon after this we saw the enemy appear right in our rear and capture the reinforcements. We were now hopelessly cut off by hundreds of the enemy, and we ourselves were shortly afterwards captured about 4pm. My sappers put up a good fight – better than many of the trained infantry – and we fought until we were surrounded and captured. From the very first we fought against great odds, and in a position which was outflanked on both sides.'[1]

'We now began our weary march back towards the German lines, passing through our own barrage on the way. There were some ghastly sights.' Ronald and his men ended up at a place near Ecourt-Saint-Quentin, ten miles away, where they were directed into a muddy field and given a small piece of brown sour bread and some coffee substitute. [2] 'This was my first bite since 8am; all I had throughout the day being a few mouthfuls of dirty water,' he said. 'Hungry as I was it took me all my time to eat my piece of bread it was so vile. That night we spent in the open field, all huddled together for warmth. It was bitterly cold, having started to freeze and a white mist having settled down. Thus ended the 21st – a day never to be forgotten – but for dog-tiredness, miserable wretchedness and coldness, worse was to follow.'

The men were forced to continue their march for a further two days, stopping in Marchiennes, close to the border with Belgium, 'in a small place', possibly a barn, where Ronald estimates about 3,000 men were 'penned up like beasts', all sleeping on straw in the freezing cold. He wrote that he wished he had his coat and regretted having discarded his vest the week before. His diary describes the food, a kind of *Sauerkraut*, as 'the most damnably vile pig-wash you could imagine' and he reckons he and his colleagues were so hungry they 'had practically sunk to the level of beasts': 'I saw men scramble and fight to get a handful of crumbs after the officers had got issued with their bread. Occasionally, the French civilians threw a turnip or pieces of bread over the wire; there was a general rush when this happened. To put it bluntly, it was absolutely concentrated hell.'

On 26 March, the men were taken by train to Belgium, then by road to Rastatt prison camp in Germany, where they arrived on 30 March. Here, they were allotted huts, given bread, coffee and a bath. Later they were given postcards to tell their loved ones they were safe, and to ask for foodstuffs and other treats to be sent to them. Ronald described that being able to tell Mary he was well was 'a great load off my mind', and the thought of the parcels she would send gave him something to look forward to, even if they might take a month to arrive. But, as Ronald fought off hunger pangs and worried about his sister, the 14-year-old girl was already beginning to receive communications suggesting that her brother was missing and probably dead. In a letter dated 2 April 1918, Major Ray Robinson of the Royal Engineers informed her that Ronald was last seen on 21 March 'very gallantly holding a piece of our line with a few of his men from his company. The enemy occupied this ground shortly afterwards and we can only hope that he was taken prisoner. I cannot tell you how sorry we are that you should have this anxiety for his safety.' In a further letter, eight days later, sent to a relative (possibly Mary's Aunt Meg), Major Robinson said he could not 'hold out any real hope of Lft Macdonald being a prisoner in the circumstances. I am very much afraid that he was killed.' The major explained that

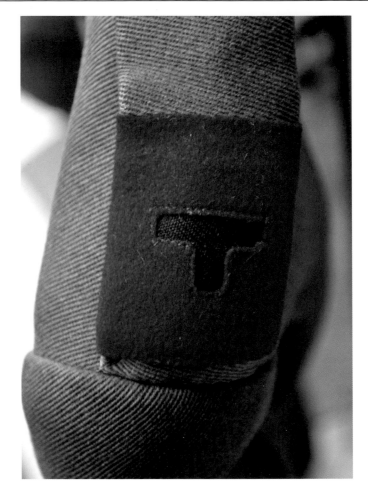

THE 'T' FROM THE EPAULETTE OF RONALD'S SERVICE DRESS JACKET
INDICATES THAT HE BELONGED TO A TUNNELLING UNIT.

letters had already been received by the families of men captured on 21 March, and
that he had written to others who were with Ronald that morning, but who were
now in hospital. He promised to keep the family informed if he heard anything.

For almost two months, Mary was given little hope that Ronald had survived the
attack – until 22 May, when a letter from the War Office said that the Postal Censor
had picked up a communication from him, stating that he was a POW. By this time,
Ronald had, in fact, sent many letters home to Mary, hoping that she and Aunt Meg
were well but mostly containing lists of requests for food and other items – including
homemade pancakes, dates, honey, tea, peppermint creams, tobacco, carbolic soap,

Oxo cubes and bread. It was many months before he received anything back, and his spirits slumped. His diary relates how he willed his name to be on the list of officers leaving for their permanent prison camp, and how one chap was shot for trying to escape. 'Many times since the 21st I wished a bullet had taken me away,' he wrote on 10 April 1918. 'I have been so cold, miserable, hungry and broken-spirited. Ah well, I suppose it is all in the fortune of war.'

Over the coming weeks, Ronald complained repeatedly about the freezing conditions, his constant hunger and his battle to keep the lice away. 'It is very cold and raw today and I haven't been warm yet. Oh, it's just a mere existence this life. The food we get keeps one alive and no more ... It is a job to keep yourself even moderately clean, having no change of underclothing and the only soap we can get won't lather.' But he perked up when mentioning his friendship with Archie Dowie, a Royal Scot from Edinburgh, and the camp's weekly church service, remembering the service held shortly after his capture at Marchiennes: 'When we prayed for those who were in anxiety at home, I felt my eyes get moist as I thought of what might have been. I shall never forget that service. We were all packed close, some standing, some sitting; officers and men, unshaven, unwashed; some hatless, some with their steel helmets on, others with the lining of their helmets stuck on their heads; some wounded, some smoking, others not so fortunate; in short, all battle scarred, all weary and all thinking of their dear ones at home and of the pals left behind on the battlefield.' He described himself as feeling 'rotten and depressed' at having been captured instead of continuing the fight. 'It is awful to know that we must stay here, helpless and unable to assist in any way, but just while away one weary monotonous day after another, praying for good news and the end of the war.'

On 1 June 1918, Ronald reported – without any form of glee – that he and his colleagues were to leave for their permanent base at Graudenz, in West Prussia, which is now part of Poland. His diary appears to end a week later, but his letters home continued. In one dated 7 July, it is clear that he had yet to receive anything from Mary, although he noted with much excitement that he had heard from their Aunt Lina, whose postcard dated 25 May only arrived on 3 July. 'By Jove I was glad to get it and to learn that you are well. It was a great relief to me I can tell you. I read and re-read the postcard until I knew it off by heart. I am expected to get a letter from you any day now. I must congratulate you Mary for passing your exams, especially when you were undergoing such an anxious time. You have done awfully well and are a plucky wee lass and no mistake.' It is clear Ronald must have heard from Mary a short while afterwards, because on 12 August Major Robinson wrote to Ronald saying how delighted he was to hear he had survived 'instead of sharing Capt Whitehead's fate'. And in a note dated 6 September, Ronald told Mary that he had only received three letters from her, all written months earlier. He added that he was pleased she was getting on well at swimming and hoped she was sticking with her music. He also mused on how tall she must be: 'I will notice a bit difference in you – I wish I could see you now,' but included a brotherly reprimand over her request for more pets: 'You surely don't want a cat in the house as well as a dog? If you have one when I come home I'm afraid I will put it out.' He admitted his mood had improved since the post started arriving. 'I feel quite different now – the result of parcels.' It is also possible that during this time Ronald was a contributor to *The Vistula*, a handwritten newspaper produced by POWs at the camp. The weekly publication was full of news from home, items on prominent prisoners, camp notes, sport, an 'in memoriam' page, in addition to illustrations, advertisements and cartoons.

In a letter dated 2 December 1918, from Ronald's pal Archie Dowie, Mary finally received the news she had been waiting for – that her beloved brother was on his way home. Archie, who had arrived at the Prisoners of War Reception Camp, South Ripon, told her that Ronald was quite well in Graudenz, and was likely to be among the next batch of prisoners to return. 'From information received on board the boat coming over I think it will be 14 to 18 days before Ronnie gets home and not 4 as was first expected,' he wrote. 'Just have patience and you will have him home for Christmas yet,' he assured her. 'He is as safe as houses and when he steps on board the Danish steamer at Danzig he is on neutral soil and the Danes treat us very well. He will have to come on here for 24 hours just to report and give information. Believe me. Yours sincerely, Archie Dowie.'

In fact, Ronald was repatriated on 18 December 1918, just in time to hear Field Marshal Sir Douglas Haig, commander-in-chief of British forces on the Western Front, pay tribute to the work of the Tunnelling Companies in a Christmas address: 'At their own special work, mine warfare, they have demonstrated their complete superiority over the Germans, and whether in the patient defensive mining, in the magnificent success at Messines, or in the preparation for the offensives of the Somme, Arras, and Ypres, they have shown the highest qualities both as military engineers and as fighting troops. Their work in the very dangerous task of removing enemy traps and delay action charges on subways, dugouts, bridging, roads and the variety of other services on which they have been engaged has been on a level with their work in the mines. They have earned the thanks of the whole army for their contribution to the defeat of the enemy.'

In May 1919, Ronald was exonerated by the Army Council from any blame for his capture, and he was formally released from duty four months later. He went on to marry Elsie McAdam, a childhood sweetheart from Glasgow, and became a lecturer on mine management at Castleford Technical College in Yorkshire, where he was later appointed president of the Mine Managers Association. The couple never had children, and Ronald died in York, in 1972, aged seventy-five.

As for his sister Mary, she married William Veitch in 1929. Her son, Ron Veitch – Ronald's nephew – said: 'My mother was only 13 when her parents died and Ronnie went missing, so it was a very difficult time for her. She idolised her brother, so you can imagine her relief when she heard he was alive and had been taken prisoner. The fact she held on to all his letters and memorabilia for such a long time shows how much she loved him. To me, an only child, Uncle Ronnie was my hero. It's hard to believe how dangerous his job was – digging tunnels under the opposing trenches, packing them with explosives, lighting the fuse and running – and then having to teach his men, who were just miners, not soldiers, to fire rifles as the Germans were advancing on them, is just incredible. He was a very brave man.'

Endnotes

1 Captain W. Grant Grieve and Bernard Newman, in *The Story of the Tunnelling Companies, Royal Engineers, During the World War*, 1936, comment on the 21 March attack: 'Most of the Tunnelling Companies became involved in the fighting, especially those sections working in advanced areas, and sustained heavy casualties. Long-established conditions changed in a day. The Tunnellers, who had been accustomed to long periods in settled billets or camps, found themselves involved in another phase of their varied career, a war of movement ... In the Bullecourt Sector, 174th Company suffered severely – one section losing two officers and thirty-seven other ranks. They were working on machine-gun emplacements, and with them was a fatigue party of about thirty machine-gunners. The whole party, under Second-Lieutenant Macdonald, acted as infantry when the assault developed, and were last seen holding a piece of line near Railway Reserve. During the next week this Company dug and wired over 9,000 yards of trench and cleared out caves at Monchy-au-Bois.'

2 By this stage of the war, the Royal Navy's blockade of Germany was biting deeply, and the quality and quantity of Germany's food supply were deteriorating all the time. The German military were given priority, over civilians (and certainly over POWs), but few were well fed, and many had to resort to substitute (*Ersatz*) foods, such as 'coffee' made from barley or other ingredients.

'Off to France'
A FAMILY FRAGMENTED

'Give this to Jeanie Cavan,' the voice shouted as a red and beige object was thrown from the train window. As the troop train rattled through Carluke station, Scotland, a small cardboard box bounced onto the platform. Inside was a folded scrap of paper with an address scribbled in ink – 'Mrs Cavan, Drill Hall, Carluke' – and the simple message: 'Dearest Wife and Bairns. Off to France. Love to you all, Daddy' and the date: 29 March 1918.

Jean was thirty-two, and four months pregnant with her fourth child, when her husband George's message came to her, via an unknown stranger. It meant that after months of training, Sergeant Major George Cavan, from the 9th (Glasgow Highlanders) Battalion, Highland Light Infantry, was finally being dispatched to France, to help stem the onslaught of the concerted German Spring Offensive, which began with Operation Michael on 21 March.

George and Jean had been married for nine years, having met in Beith, Ayrshire, at the church where they both worshipped. George, who was born in the town on 31 July 1882, never knew his father, an Irish engine-fireman also called George, who died when he was just a few months old. His mother, Janet, married again, but she died when George was just ten years old, leaving him in the care of an aunt whose large family also lived in Beith. After leaving school, George joined the Highland Light Infantry in Glasgow, initially serving in India and then Egypt. It was during

THE MATCHBOX CONTAINING GEORGE CAVAN'S FINAL MESSAGE TO HIS FAMILY, AS RETRIEVED FROM CARLUKE STATION IN MARCH 1918.

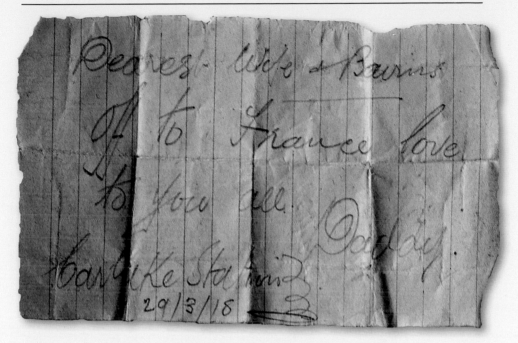

one of his trips home that George met Jean Taylor. The couple were married on 12 December 1909, when George was 27 and Jean was 23.

George and his new wife were initially posted to Cork in Ireland, but they returned to Scotland a year later, with their first child on the way. They moved into the Drill Hall Army accommodation in Carluke, Lanarkshire, where George was tasked with training Territorial forces. Their son William was born in January 1911, followed by a daughter, Jean, in April 1913. George's army duties often took him away from home and sometimes the family travelled with him. Tragically, on one of these trips in 1915 William became very ill and died a few days later, possibly from appendicitis or kidney failure. In June 1916, Jean gave birth to another daughter, Lucy.

George's family say he was constantly frustrated in his desire to go to France to fight, so it was not until March 1918 – eight months before the war ended – that his wish was realised. Away at a training camp in Scotland, the orders came through that George and his soldiers were to be dispatched to the Western Front. It was as his troop train was passing through Carluke station that he scribbled the note, stuffed it into a matchbox and threw it onto the platform. Little did anyone know it would contain the sergeant major's final words to his family. On 13 April 1918, the young NCO was killed in action at the Battle of Hazebrouck, just days after arriving at the front in France.

George arrived at a nail-biting moment on the front line, during the second German offensive of the spring – Operation Georgette – also known as the Battle of the Lys, in which German forces attempted a decisive breakthrough in Flanders, beginning in the first week of April. The 9th Battalion, which formed part of the 33rd Division, was particularly heavily engaged between 12 and 15 April, in the fighting around Hazebrouck. Only two days before George died, and with the high ground of Messines just lost to the Germans, Field Marshal Sir Douglas Haig had issued his celebrated 'Special Order of the Day' – commonly referred to as his 'Backs to the Wall' communiqué to the British Armies in France. He recognised the seriousness of the situation and urged his men to keep strong: 'There is no other course open to us but to fight it out. Every position must be held to the last man: there must be no retirement. With our backs to the wall and believing in the justice of our cause, each one of us must fight on to the end. The safety of our homes and the freedom of mankind alike depend upon the conduct of each one of us at this critical moment.' The Allies lost further ground, yet managed to rally, and by the end of the month the German offensive

◀

A PHOTOGRAPH OF JEAN CAVAN, SHOWING
HER IN HER LATE TWENTIES.

▼

ONE SIDE OF JEAN CAVAN'S
MUCH-TREASURED LOCKET,
BEARING THE PICTURE
OF GEORGE.

BRITISH CASUALTIES, TEMPORARILY BLINDED BY GAS, AWAIT TREATMENT AT THE START
OF THE GERMANS' OPERATION GEORGETTE OFFENSIVE.

ran out of momentum and halted, its objective of a breakthrough still unachieved.

By a cruel stroke of fate, news of George's death reached Carluke before Jean
was officially notified. Jean's grand-daughter, Maureen Rogers, said the family
understood that the first she heard was when a woman in the street stopped her
to commiserate. Disbelieving her, Jean shouted at the woman, accusing her of
telling lies and spreading rumours. She ran home only to find officers from George's
regiment waiting for her, to confirm the news.

George is commemorated on the Ploegsteert Memorial near Ypres. A few
possessions – his wedding ring, wallet with a few coins and his Boy's Brigade medal –
were eventually returned to Jean. In the evenings after George's death, her children
recall watching their mother sit quietly, brushing her long hair and crying. From
then on she always wore a locket close to her heart. On one side of it was a photo of
George; on the other a picture of her at the time she lost him.

At first the family was allowed to stay on at the Drill Hall, where Jean gave
birth to Georgina in September 1918. During this time, the grieving widow had to
cope with little Jean contracting scarlet fever, and Lucy suffering severe whooping
cough. Eventually, the family moved out to a small house in the centre of Carluke,
with Jean having to survive on a widow's pension of just £2 and 2 shillings and

JEAN CAVAN WITH HER THREE
DAUGHTERS, TWO YEARS AFTER GEORGE DIED.

sixpence a week. But in 1922, the family set sail on SS *Balranald* to start a new life in Australia. Jean's aunt had already emigrated with her husband and two children, in 1920, and was living in a Soldier's Settlement in Red Cliffs, Victoria, where they were given a block of desert land, on delayed repayment terms, to turn into a fruit-growing area. After a voyage of at least five weeks, Jean's family arrived in Melbourne and then boarded a train to Red Cliffs, over 320 miles north-west of the city.

Initially, the family stayed with Jean's aunt and uncle, with little Jean and Lucy attending school in a disused shearing shed; but eventually they moved into their own home on the edge of town. Jean bought a piece of land for a few pounds and the family put up three tents for sleeping and two canvas 'humpies' – or temporary shelters – for living. Cooking was done outside on a camp oven sunk into the ground, with Jean catering not only for her family, but also for the workmen building an extension to the railway. According to a journal written by Lucy, all three girls contracted 'sandy blight' – a serious eye infection – and Lucy suffered an illness that left her unable to walk for some weeks.

After two years, though, Jean decided they should return to Scotland, and the family came back to settle in Helensburgh, in Argyll and Bute, close to Jean's youngest brother. The four of them lived in a flat on the top floor of a four-storey building, above shops at ground level, but with a view over the River Clyde. The accommodation was small, comprising a bedroom with a fireplace, a sitting room with a recessed bed, a hall with another bed, a tiny bathroom and a kitchen with a table, a coal range and bunker. There were also pulleys on the ceiling to hang the washing if it was raining. The laundry was done in the basement, with each flat having a designated washing day for using the copper basin with a fire beneath, the scrubbing board and the wringer. Jean's bed was in the kitchen – a high affair with room underneath for storing suitcases and baskets. She began work as a night nurse one-mile's walk away, caring for an elderly stroke patient in her own home. Jean did this work for 9 years, working 50 weeks a year, 6 nights a week from 9pm to 9am, on a weekly wage of 30 shillings.

Jean finally retired when her children left home – Jean to be married, Georgie to work further afield, and Lucy, who suffered from tuberculosis, to a sanatorium where she met her

A PRINCESS MARY GIFT BOX KEPT BY JEAN. THESE TINS, CONTAINING TOBACCO AND OTHER TREATS, WERE DISTRIBUTED TO BRITISH AND IMPERIAL SERVICEMEN AT CHRISTMAS 1914.

husband, also a TB survivor. Lucy and her husband moved to Australia in 1949, followed by her mother and her sister Georgie in 1954. Jean, who never remarried, would always talk of her soldier George with lasting love and affection. It was a love that did not stretch to the army. As her daughters grew up and Armistice Day was fervently commemorated, Jean could bear no talk of war and glory. Instead, she would wash blankets and clean the house – anything to shut out the sadness and memories of what could have been. She claimed that the matchbox with George's final message to the family was her most important possession. That, and the locket she wore until her death, in 1964, of pancreatic cancer.

George and Jean's grand-daughter Maureen Rogers said: 'The message from George was the most important thing in my grandmother's life. The couple didn't have that much time together, but there is no doubt he was the centre of her world. She never remarried and did her best to bring up three daughters in extraordinary circumstances. I am very honoured to have the matchbox, which is an extraordinary link to the past and a wonderful tangible piece of history.'[1]

Endnotes

1 At the time of writing, Maureen Rogers – who lives in Sydney, Australia – was planning to give the matchbox and other mementoes from George's life to the museum of the Royal Highland Fusiliers, the regiment created by the merging in 1959 of the Royal Scots Fusiliers and the Highland Light Infantry.

'We were really hungry, ravenous'

NEVER SAYING DIE – IN LOVE OR WAR

As shells and bullets rained down, Fred Heley's captain looked up gingerly out of the trenches. He quickly ducked back down again. 'My God the Germans are all round us,' he said. 'There's Germans everywhere I look ... We're surrounded!' Unlike the other three companies of Fred's battalion, which had received orders to retire, his had heard nothing. 'The company I were in, I suppose the telephone were blowed up – we never had no orders – we were on our own. The others retired and we didn't. You couldn't retire unless you've got orders, you see,' remembered Fred, in an interview almost seventy years later. 'Well they captured the whole company – 200 men – and I were one of them.'

And that was Fred's introduction to the front line. The young lad from Stewkley, Buckinghamshire, who had worked with horses at a remount depot as a teenager, had only joined the army the year before, in May 1917, when he turned eighteen.[1] He was posted to the Royal Warwickshire Regiment's headquarters in Warwick, and then up to Northumberland for training until March 1918, when he was given 14 days' embarkation leave before heading to war. But before he boarded the train home, his leave was cancelled, and instead the teenager found himself *en route* to Dover. Gone were visions of his mother's beefsteak pudding back in Stewkley, or a night out with Winifred Lizzie Mead, the girl he had been courting since they met at Stewkley School. 'I can't think of any other soldier that ever was posted abroad without embarkation leave,' said Fred.[2] Within 48 hours of arriving in Dover, he was 'up the line' on the Western Front, defending against the 1918 Spring Offensive – the all-out (and last) German effort to win the war.

WINIFRED LIZZIE MEAD,
AGED ABOUT 18 YEARS

FRED HELEY IN UNIFORM, DURING HIS SERVICE
IN EGYPT, 1919.

It seems that Fred found himself caught up in the Battle of Estaires, which opened with the heavy bombardment of the line between Béthune and Armentières on 9 April. This was the beginning of the second German offensive that spring, 'Operation Georgette', intended to smash the predominantly British positions around Ypres and drive on to the Channel coast. To start with, things went very badly for the Allies. The action at Estaires, ending on 11 April, saw the Allied Portuguese forces collapse under the German pressure: the 20,000-strong 2nd Portuguese Division lost about 300 officers and 7,000 men killed, wounded or captured.

Fred said that the men in his battalion had been in reserve to the Portuguese, who were by now completely exhausted and demoralised. The Portuguese were fleeing – and Fred and his comrades were captured. 'Things were very, very difficult for England just then. If I remember right, they over run us. They got to Brussels; they were well on their way to Paris, and I were captured. [3] Them that captured me said: "We should be in London in a month – you know that, don't you?" Well, I couldn't help but agree with them because they were doing just what they liked with us. Well, there were dead and wounded laying everywhere. So our job then, for perhaps ten days or something, were backwards and forwards, picking up the wounded and taking them to the dressing stations. They were all German – we weren't allowed to pick our own up. And I could never remember having a meal. We were working day and night, day and night, picking them – there were hundreds of them about there.'

Fed up with no sleep, little food and his relentless role as stretcher-bearer for his German captors, Fred hatched a plan to escape. 'I said to my mate who was helping with this stretcher: "I've had enough of this – I'm going to see if I can get away and

FRED HELEY (*FAR RIGHT, SEATED*), WITH THE MANCHESTER REGIMENT, DURING POSTWAR SERVICE IN EGYPT, 1919.

get a sleep." He said: "Don't be a fool." I said: "Won't you come with me?" And he said: "No, they'll shoot you." Well I said: "They'll shoot you when you've done what they want you to." I begged at him to come, but he wouldn't. And one night, in the very thick of a barrage – there were shells falling all over everywhere – I hopped it and went for cover. All on me own. So I've got to find food, but what I wanted more than anything else was sleep. Well, I daren't come out in the daylight. I were sheltering in the old trenches, in the 1915–16 trenches that were in German hands then. But they'd been in English hands for the big battles where Ypres and Armentières had been fought years before. But I managed to get something: farmhouses (that) were blown to

WIN AND FRED AT THEIR MARRIAGE IN 1964, AT THE WESLEYAN METHODIST CHAPEL, STEWKLEY.

pieces – I didn't do too bad. But it got more difficult you see and I could only come out when it was dark 'cos if the Germans had seen me, they'd lock me up again. This is all a guess – perhaps after two to three weeks – they got me again, and then the fun started with me. They said I were a spy. I couldn't make 'em believe that I were captured ... so I had to go in front of officers for interrogation. They really thought I were a spy, although I were in uniform. Anyway, they found out that I wasn't a spy, that what I'd been telling them was the truth, but they really couldn't understand why I'd got away the two or three weeks without them finding me.'

Fred was held captive for eight months, but the only message his mother received was from the War Office. It was a message that devastated Fred's girlfriend Winifred, according to her great-niece Jill Scott. 'Win said that when Mrs Heley had received notification that Fred was missing, presumed dead and then nothing more was heard of or from him, they assumed the worst had happened. By that time 34 lads from Stewkley had been killed, so bad news was frequently received in the village.'

While his family and sweetheart were mourning his loss, Fred spent the next eight months in captivity, digging fall-back trenches for the Germans, and transporting barbed wire. 'I never got out of the firing line,' he said. 'Our food were terrible, what they called goulash – that's pickled vegetables. [4] I don't think the whole time I were there I had any protein, butter, cheese, nothing on bread. We had one loaf between three of us and a bowl of soup. We were really hungry, ravenous. We were so hungry that when the war were over we were all took to an isolation camp between Dover and London and they kept us there for three weeks or a month because the doctors kept saying our stomach had got no lining. I come back to England with the same shirt on as what I went 18 months before – and it had never been washed. One of the main things up the trenches and in the camps were lice. They'd got nothing to kill them. We were filthy.'

Back on English soil, Fred was given a printed card to send his family, to tell them he was alive and coming home. His mother later said: 'That's the first word we heard from you all the time you were in France.' According to Jill Scott that letter caused Win consternation. 'She had been nursing a broken heart after she heard that Fred was missing, presumed dead. However, another soldier, Stephen Bachell, who had been blinded in his right eye, had been sent to recuperate with relatives in Stewkley, and Win struck up a friendship with him. As the end of the war was celebrated, they became engaged.'

After his convalescence, Fred was put on a train bound for Leighton Buzzard, not knowing what may have befallen his parents or girlfriend since he last heard from them. But as luck would have it, at the very moment he began the five-mile walk home from Leighton Buzzard to Stewkley, he met his sweetheart Winifred taking relatives to the station in a horse and cart. On the way back she picked him up. 'I thought "you ain't very excited,"' said Fred, recalling the reunion. 'Well, while we were coming home, she said: "I thought you were killed. I'm engaged to another soldier."' She then continued: '"We'll be friends, won't we?" "Oh yes," I said, "Yes, we'll be friends." We were very good friends. But one thing she said: "I've got a very nice girlfriend and I'll introduce you to her." She did – and I married her.'

Fred asked Winifred to drop him at the bottom of the village, so he could walk up to his parents' home. Meanwhile, she went on ahead and let everyone know her former love was back. 'As he passed their houses, parents brought their children out to the roadside to bash saucepans with wooden spoons and to cheer and wave him up the high street,' said Jill Scott, who was told the story by her grandmother, Winifred's elder sister Ella. 'It was an emotional homecoming for Fred, his family and villagers.'

Fred was on leave for only a short time when he was dispatched to Egypt in 1919 for two years, as part of the Manchester Regiment. He married Ethel May Tattam in 1925, while Winifred married Stephen in 1921 and moved to London. Fred took over his father's carrying business, collecting villagers' orders from the local towns and acting as a rural bus or taxi. He became the first person in Stewkley to own a lorry. During the Second World War he had a job transporting German POWs from their camp near his marital home in Drayton Parslow to nearby farms, where they worked. 'I made some very good friends with them, because I knew a little bit of German. I'd got a little bit of pity for them I think because they didn't know nothing about their families much. Some of them had been away for two years.'

Fred and Winifred both had happy marriages, yet neither couple had children. In 1960 Stephen died and Winifred moved back to live with Jill's family in Stewkley. 'I loved having her live with us as she was such fun and brought with her such metropolitan wonders as a "stereo radiogram",' said Jill. 'We would sit in her room listening to her records – she was very in tune with young people.' Fred's wife Ethel passed away in 1961 and he quickly discovered Winifred was back living in the neighbouring village. 'After his wife died, Fred and Win would meet at village and chapel events and eventually became engaged,' said Jill. The childhood sweethearts were married at the Wesleyan Methodist Chapel in Stewkley in 1964. 'Fred and Win were a very jolly couple,' said Jill. 'They were great companions for each other and enjoyed their last years together, until Winifred died in 1980.'

Fred died in 1994, having spent his final years in quiet reflection. 'Fred was a stoical chap and had great inner strength,' said Jill. 'These qualities and his genial manner enabled him to endure and survive his experiences in the Great War, then accept the loss of his girlfriend without any lingering bitterness. That he and Win should quietly hold a flame for each other through the years was a testament to their love, with their eventual marriage being a fittingly romantic conclusion to their story.'

Endnotes

1 'Remount depot' – the Army Remount Service depots acted as collecting points for horses from farms, businesses, hunts and riding stables. The service, originating in Queen Victoria's reign, was massively expanded during the First World War, reflecting the enormous demand for horses – for the cavalry and officers, to haul wagons and guns, and to carry supplies.
2 It was indeed highly unusual for a war-bound

soldier not to receive embarkation leave.
3 Fred was incorrect about Brussels – it had fallen in 1914 – but Paris was indeed threatened by the German offensives of 1918, coming within shelling range, though never occupied by the enemy.
4 'Goulash' – more likely to be *Sauerkraut*, the German dish of finely-sliced and pickled green cabbage, though a stew is also possible.

'Adventurous people'
FROM CAIRO TO THE WESTERN FRONT

It was a strange sort of pilgrimage. The First World War had only ended the year before when Oxford graduate Harold Edwin Hurst, his wife Winifred, and her teenage niece Nancy set off for France and Belgium, to locate the graves of lost relatives and friends. Harold and Winifred had travelled from Cairo, where they rented an apartment following their marriage in 1912. Nancy, meanwhile, had taken time out from her studies as a social science student at the University of

CHARLES AND ELLEN HAWES (*CIRCLED ON THE PHOTO*), WORKING TOGETHER AT THE ENGLISH HOSPITAL, NEVERS, FRANCE, *c*.1914.

London. The 19-year-old was almost certainly the driver among this strange trio, because she was mad about cars. While Harold was used to driving in remote parts of the Sudan and Uganda as part of his job as a hydrologist on the River Nile, he refused to take the wheel in Europe, following an accident in France before the war. Winifred, a well-read, cultured and – according to her family – slightly eccentric woman, who had never worked, would have dismissed the very idea of driving as absurd. But as the group motored through Flanders and Picardy, the sadness of their journey and the devastation of the landscape around them must have been overwhelming. For Nancy the trip was particularly poignant. Her beloved father, Charles Hawes – Winifred's brother – had been killed by a sea mine close to Le Havre in 1917, and two of her maternal uncles had died the year before.

Born in 1900, Nancy was the middle of Charles and Ellen Hawes's three children, and the only girl between Ben and Ernest. She was her father's favourite and often joined him on his rounds as a country doctor, visiting patients in a pony and trap. It was a privileged, Edwardian upbringing in a family that loved sport and service to the community. But in 1912 that idyll was shattered. Without explanation, Ellen took her children to live in Switzerland. According to the family, the surprise move to Lausanne followed Ellen's discovery that Charles 'had developed a sudden passion' for the children's young Swedish nanny, who worked at their home in Pangbourne. Within six months of arriving, though, Ellen returned home alone, leaving Ben at a boarding school, and her two younger children in the care of a headmistress of the local state school. It was the start of a period that saw the youngsters being brought up by many strangers.

The three Hawes siblings returned from Switzerland in the spring of 1914. By the time war broke out, their parents were reunited, although no-one knows whether they were completely reconciled. Instead, they threw their energies into starting up a hospital in Nevers, on the Loire, in central France, rallying local people to donate bedclothes and anything useful to help them. Once there, Ellen carried out the dispensary and secretarial work as a nurse for the VADs (Voluntary Aid Detachments), while Charles took over as chief doctor and became a captain in the Royal Army Medical Corps (RAMC). However, their work together was short-lived. In January 1915, Charles returned to England to join a hospital ship, which went on to take the wounded from the front in Gallipoli to Alexandria.[1] He was then transferred to a similar vessel, HMHS *Lanfranc*, which ferried the wounded from the battlefields in northern France back to England.[2] At the time, daughter Nancy

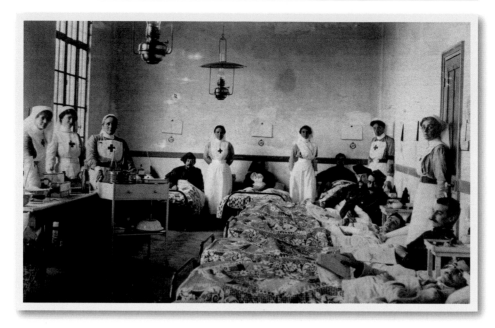

ELLEN HAWES (*FAR RIGHT, BY DOOR*) ON THE WARD AT NEVERS,
WITH HER PATIENTS AND COLLEAGUES.

was living with a district nurse in Pangbourne and went to school at Queen Anne's, Caversham. In her unpublished autobiography, 'The House by the Side of the Road', she recalled how shocked she was to hear that Secretary of State for War Lord Kitchener had drowned at sea, along with the father of three of her schoolmates. [3] It was a fate that was to befall Nancy's father less than a year later.

Having served as a surgeon on *Lanfranc*, Charles was posted to HMHS *Salta*, a steamship requisitioned as a hospital ship to transport injured soldiers from Le Havre to Southampton. As hospital trains, ambulances and wounded men on stretchers awaited her arrival at Le Havre on 10 April 1917, the ship struck a mine at the entrance to the port, causing a huge explosion that breached the hull near the engine room. As the ship listed and began to sink, a British patrol boat, *P-26*, tried to come alongside to assist, but also struck a mine and sank. [4] Of the 205 people on board the *Salta*, 9 nurses, 79 crew and 42 members of the RAMC were killed – among them Nancy's father, Captain Godfrey Charles Brown Hawes, aged fifty. According to Nancy's son, Stephen Hurst, the 17-year-old found out about her father's death shortly after arriving home from school. 'She was hanging up her hat and coat when the door bell rang,' he said. 'As she opened the door she was confronted with the uniform that was feared by every family in the land – it was the telegraph boy delivering telegrams. Immediately, Nancy knew what that telegram contained. It was the War Office message announcing the death of her father.'

By this time, Nancy's mother Ellen was serving as a VAD nurse in London, and the news must have been devastating. The 50-year-old, who had already lost two brothers in the Anglo-Boer War (1899–1902), was still reeling from the deaths the previous year of two of her remaining siblings, on the Western Front. One, Donald Lewis, commanded 2nd Wing, Royal Flying Corps, and was flying a Morane Parasol – a fragile two-seater reconnaissance aircraft – when he was shot down east of Wytschaete, on 10 April 1916. The other, Harold Lewis, was shot with his dog on the infamous first day of the Battle of the Somme (1 July 1916), as he walked forward with the remaining men of 20th Battalion, Manchester Regiment (the 5th Manchester Pals) at Fricourt Wood.

Ellen's VAD records reveal that two months after her husband's death she was demoted from her role as staff nurse to cook. Stephen Hurst said it was possible that the combination of having to deal with badly wounded and dying soldiers on a daily basis, plus the loss of four brothers and then her husband, might have caused his grandmother to have a breakdown or to request a transfer.

All these memories must have played on the minds of Nancy, Harold and Winifred, during their road trip to the old front line in 1919. Afterwards, the three resumed their former lives – Harold and Winifred went home to Cairo, while Nancy returned to her studies in London. Harold, who was a senior official in the Ministry of Nile Control during First World War, also continued his work making spare parts for the British Army. He had been developing a 'hyperscope' for firing over the trench parapet – a device that combined rifle, gun-sight, periscope and trigger mechanism – but such was his perfectionism that it was not finished before the war ended. He also enjoyed creating household furnishings out of unusual objects, including a lamp-stand made out of a piece of an RFC aircraft propeller, and a dinner gong that combined the tooth of a Nile hippo he had shot (to feed his porters in the Sudan) with the brass shell case taken by an officer friend from the German cruiser *Goeben* in the Dardanelles. [5] The gong was used by the Hursts' Berber servants to call the family to dinner. During the early war years, Harold had also got to know fellow Oxford graduate T.E. Lawrence – 'Lawrence of Arabia' – who was working as an intelligence officer for the British Army in Egypt. 'My dad invited him over to supper on a number of occasions, but he never came – he was

HAROLD HURST'S UNUSUAL
WARTIME SOUVENIR: A DINNER
GONG MADE FROM A HIPPO TOOTH
AND THE SHELL CASING FROM THE
GERMAN CRUISER *GOEBEN*.

a lonely sort of fellow,' said Stephen Hurst.

A few years after the war, the Hursts moved into a large house at Bulaq Dakrur, an oasis about six miles from Cairo. The couple were known for their joyful dinner parties; while Harold played the piano, Winifred would sing and dance. However, in 1926, Winifred fell terminally ill with leukaemia, and Harold asked Nancy to come out to Egypt to nurse her aunt, who died later that year. Nancy, who at the age of 26 had almost given up hope of finding a husband because 'there was a great shortage of men' after the war, stayed on to act as Harold's housekeeper and organiser. The couple grew closer and married in Cairo's Roman Catholic cathedral in 1928. While Nancy, then aged 28, was a Protestant and Harold, 48, an atheist, the Church of England refused to marry them because of the laws of consanguinity. However, after the birth of their son, Stephen, in February 1932, they went through a marriage service for a second time at a church in Guildford, Surrey, and went on to have a second son, Andy, who was born in 1935.

The family was evacuated to England in the summer of 1939, eventually settling in Oxford; but as the Second World War started, Harold was called back to Egypt by the Colonial Office, because they mistakenly believed he was a medical doctor, rather than a doctor in physics. Nancy, meanwhile, opened the family home as a shelter to a stream of refugees from concentration camps and evacuees from London. Harold eventually retired from his post as director general of the Ministry of Irrigation in 1966, after 60 years' continuous service for the Egyptian government.[6] He died just days short of his 99th birthday in December

1978. Nancy's mother Ellen died in 1957, while Nancy herself suffered a mental breakdown during the early 1950s and died in 1989, aged eighty-nine.

Stephen Hurst, a sculptor, said: 'My Mum was a remarkable person, and like her own mother, Ellen, had a very hard life because of two world wars. They both loved helping others, which could be a trial to the family at times, and neither of them was easy to live with. Ellen remains an enigma to me. I know she was a stoical and conscientious person with a massive social conscience, but none of my family had the faintest idea until recently that she had been a VAD through the war or ever spoke about her experiences. My parents' relationship was not a love-match; while Nancy had a great respect for Harold, she married him to have children and because all the eligible men in her life were dead. But both were adventurous people who loved travelling. Had Nancy not accompanied her Uncle Harold and Aunt Winnie on that journey along the Western Front in 1919, I would not be here today.'

Endnotes

1 The Gallipoli campaign, which began in April 1915 and lasted until January 1916, was the Allies' unsuccessful attempt to wrest the sea route between the Mediterranean and the Black Sea, via the Dardanelles Straits, from Turkey.

2 His Majesty's Hospital Ship (HMHS) *Lanfranc* was hit on 17 April 1917 by a German torpedo from the submarine *UB-40* while en route from Le Havre to Southampton. Forty lives were lost.

3 The shocking death of Lord Kitchener occurred when HMS *Hampshire*, on a diplomatic mission to Russia, hit a German mine off the Orkney Islands in June 1916 (*see* pages 64–9).

4 HMHS *Salta* had been painted white with a broad horizontal green band with red crosses, which under the Hague Convention of 1894 should have protected her from attack. She left Southampton with *Lanfranc*, *Western Australia* and an escort of destroyers on 9/10 April 1917 *en route* for Le Havre. Mines, laid the previous day by U-boat *UC-26*, were spotted drifting in the approach to Le Havre and a warning was sent

out to all vessels entering the port. Nevertheless, the ship drifted fatally into the danger zone.

5 The German battle-cruiser *Goeben*, with the light cruiser *Breslau*, played a notable role in the war. Right at the beginning, in August 1914, they evaded superior British and French naval forces in the Mediterranean to make their way to (still neutral) Turkey. The two ships were then given to the Turkish navy, along with their crews, as part of the increasingly warm German–Turkish relationship. At the end of October 1914, both ships were bombarding Russia's Black Sea ports, heralding Turkey's entry into the war on the side of the Central Powers.

6 It is after the hydrological studies carried out by Harold in his long and eminent career that the 'Hurst phenomenon' was named. He was looking for a way to model the levels of the Nile so that architects could construct an appropriately-sized reservoir system. His theory has since been used in other fields, such as economics, electronics and climatology.

'To dad's little Ghislaine'
THE FRENCH LIEUTENANT'S DAUGHTER

French Lieutenant Charles Grauss's way of coping with the trials of war was to create images of what he saw – from sketches of his comrades wearing gas masks, digging trenches or taking instructions, to pencil drawings of the places where he stayed, watercolours of the countryside and photographs of those who were killed during the conflict. Few subjects escaped his artistic eye. Charles was serving in the 339th Infantry Regiment when he made his 50-page scrapbook, which shows men, and occasionally nurses, resting, eating or simply posing; there is even a comical painting of a soldier – possibly a self-portrait – before and after a haircut and moustache trim. The illustrated diary-like account, which is interspersed with the occasional poem, including one to an unknown soldier, focused on some of the darker moments of his experience, with photos of crosses on graves and a newspaper clipping announcing his mother's death. However, it also touched on his strong Christian faith – with images of churches and cuttings about Bible lectures – which dominated his childhood.

Charles's Protestant family were originally from the Alsace region of eastern France, on the border with Germany. He was born in Nancy to Jean Georges Grauss and his wife, Julie Boss, on 31 August 1881. He studied at Nancy's School of Economics and Faculty of Law, and became active in the local Christian Union. In 1906 he was appointed general secretary of the French Christian Federation of Students and helped to organise

▶

CHARLES GRAUSS, IN UNIFORM.

CHARLES GRAUSS'S LETTER OF 18 APRIL 1916 TO HIS YOUNG DAUGHTER, GHISLAINE, BEARING SKETCHES OF THEM BOTH AT THE TOP, AND CONCLUDING WITH A PICTURE OF HIM HOLDING HER AND SENDING 'A BIG KISS'.

ILLUSTRATIONS OF TRENCH LIFE AND THE LANDSCAPES HE ENCOUNTERED,
FROM CHARLES'S SCRAPBOOK.

their summer camps for school and university pupils, which took place on the island of Oléron, off the French Atlantic coast. Charles was also a founder member of the French Scouting movement, and by 1910 he was joint general secretary of the YMCA – Young Men's Christian Association.

It was while working in an office that he met and married Elisabeth Amélie Meyer in La Rochelle on 29 May 1911, and soon afterwards the couple had a daughter, Ghislaine. The arrival of a little girl had a lasting effect on Charles, and she was never far from his thoughts when he was garrisoned with his comrades in France during the First World War. Initially Charles was part of the 26th Infantry Regiment, but during the war he served with the 339th Infantry Regiment, where he also used his artistic skills to carve and paint a number of miniature farm animals for Ghislaine to play with. [1] Charles also sent a poignant and touching letter, dated 18 April 1916, to the youngster: in this 'Letter to Dad's little Ghislaine', he painted a watercolour of himself with his daughter, depicted as a toddler, with the caption 'Dad likes Ghissou'; underneath he painted a 'wise duck' and 'Mrs Moon', a dog, and the beautiful house he wanted to give Ghislaine's mother. It concludes with a big kiss and picture of him as a soldier cuddling the daughter he was missing so much.

However, Charles was never able to see his daughter's reaction to the toys or hear what she thought about the letter. His regiment was involved in the Oise–Aisne offensive in August 1918 as, all along the Western Front, Allied armies mounted attacks. This was all part of the highly fluid Hundred Days Offensive that would eventually force the Germans back and lead to the Armistice. However, during the fighting around Juvigny in northern France on 29 August, Charles suffered a serious injury. He later died in the ambulance at Jaulzy, north of Paris, aged thirty-six.

No-one knows how the news affected Elisabeth, or what Ghislaine was told about her father. However, Charles's memory lives on at the Memorial de Verdun, the French museum dedicated to the Battle of Verdun (1916) and the wider war. A priest who knew the family donated Charles' scrapbook, the toys for Ghislaine and Charles's letter to the museum, where they continue to be displayed as a poignant reminder of the enormous price so many men paid in the conflict. In the view of historian Dr Stephen Bull, this was a fitting location for the mementoes of Charles's life: 'The 339th Infantry were at the cataclysmic battle of Verdun from June 1916 ... arguably a life or death struggle for France. The remarkable Memorial de Verdun museum occupies the site of what was once Fleury Station, at the epicentre of the battle at that time. It may be this that makes such a strong connection between Charles Grauss and the city.' [2]

But beneath the clamour of great events lies the quieter family tragedies, embodied, in Charles Grauss's case, in the images and artefacts he left behind – as Dr Bull described them, 'exquisite, sad and hopeful at the same time'.

Endnotes

1 The set of surviving animals, contained in a metal box, includes a pig, a donkey, a rabbit, a dog, a mouse, a sheep, a duck and a hen.

2 Dr Bull attended the Europeana 1914–18 roadshow at Luxembourg, when Charles Grauss's items were brought in.

'A lucky boy'

SAVED BY A FRENCH SURGEON

As Private George Richards assessed the open countryside that he and his comrades were about to cross, he spotted a German observation balloon and knew they were in trouble.[1] 'The general of HQ didn't have the commonsense to send the aircraft to bring it down – they knew we'd be trapped,' he said. 'The major looked at me and I looked at him and he said: "I know what you're thinking son – you're thinking about those idiots – so am I." I was seeing men falling all around me ... and I was saying to myself: "I've seen two of my pals killed – shelled." I was going to say "any ... minute ... now...," but before I could say "... now," Whoop – I was blown out of existence – I'd had it.' The blast knocked George unconscious, and by the time he came round, all his pals had gone. 'I thought my leg was blown off – I was too scared,' he remembered. 'I felt my leg was there; I started taking off my putties and the stretcher bearers come along.' As they removed his trousers and examined

GEORGE RICHARDS WITH HIS WIFE HARRIET,
ON THEIR WEDDING DAY IN 1928.

the injury, one of them commented: 'I don't know how the hell you're going to get back', because George's leg was broken. George observed that 'one of my men, a bullet had missed his eye; the other one had a bit of shrapnel in his toe,' and these wounded men said: 'We'll get him back.'

For a mile George hobbled with the support of his two injured comrades, and then they spotted a padre and three Red Cross men standing in a sunken road, some distance from the front line. The sight caused George to lose his temper and to threaten the group with a Mills bomb. [2] Believing they should be nearer the action and tending to the wounded, he pointed at the padre and said: 'Three days ago you were preaching to us, telling us not to be afraid of death. God would save us. And you, as our padre – you see this – if you don't go you're going to get this.' George 'had no intention of throwing it mind, but they thought I was going to do it. I hadn't finished the sentence and they ran. I said: "You should be downright ashamed of yourself."'

George and his colleagues stumbled on until they were met by medics pushing a stretcher on wheels. 'It was perishing cold – in a sense it was doing me good because the cold were neutralising the pain. They put me on the stretcher and they took us right back to the dispatch centre to get first aid. When I got there, the first thing they did was to throw a Jerry overcoat over me because my trousers had gone and I would've perished it was that cold.' Three ambulances were transporting the wounded out on a ratio of three Allies to one German; but as the last vehicle was about to leave with four Germans on board, George moved his arm revealing his shoulder badges. A medic saw the Welsh dragon emblem on his sleeve, prompting him to demand: 'Get one of those Jerries out and put Taffy in.'

George was injured on 8 October 1918, during the two-day-long Second Battle of Cambrai – part of the final Allied advance of the war, dubbed the Hundred Days Offensive. [3] In an interview with the Imperial War Museum many decades later he talked about going in to cover the flank of the Canadians there, in a battle that involved tanks and proved an overwhelming Allied success. By this time, George, a South Wales miner, had been in France about seven weeks. Born in Pembroke in August 1897, the son of Esther Richards, George never met his father, and he was brought up by his grandfather Thomas Richards, a master builder whom he worshipped. However, when his granddad died of cancer following an injury at work and his mother married a miner, Sidney Phillips, George reckoned his life was ruined. He blamed Sidney for preventing him from getting a grammar school education and for taking him out of Pembroke dockyard – dashing his hopes of becoming a shipwright – when the family moved to Cymer Afan, near Port Talbot.

George was 17 years old when war broke out, and like many Welshmen he was driven to enlist by the rhetoric of David Lloyd George – soon to be Minister of Munitions, and later prime minister – who wanted to see a Welsh army in the field; he was also spurred by the thoughts of adventures that would follow. 'I wasn't a warmonger – I don't believe in war,' said George. 'We thought we were fighting the war to end all wars and we thought ... it would be over by Christmas, and it would've been if we'd had good generals.' He tried to join up in Port Talbot, but a friend of his stepfather said he was too young. Eventually, he enlisted with the South Wales Borderers in February 1916 and became a Lewis gunner. [4] Later he boasted that miners had been a perfect fit for the rigours of army life and for fighting the Germans because of their high levels of fitness, which was especially useful when it came to digging trenches. 'I could tell a miner straight away – he was like an electric machine; other men were more like gardeners,' he said. 'We were brought up to stand up to something like that by working in the mines; and Lloyd George, he picked the right army when he picked a lot of miners.'

After Cambrai, George was sent by ambulance train to Le Havre for surgery to repair the damage to his left thigh and knee, and he was attended by a senior female nurse who, he was told, had been wounded four times. 'When we got out at Le Havre, there were these titled ladies offering us bars of chocolate. I said: "You're not patronising me. Take your chocolate. If you want to do something worthwhile for this war – do what that lady's doing." They took me up to Le Havre hospital and luck was with me all the way. I had an X-ray and the next day after that an operation.' As he was wheeled down a corridor *en route* to surgery, George said he noticed there was an operating theatre for the British and another for the French. As his was the last procedure of the day and there was a French surgeon available, he was taken into the French theatre. 'After the operation and when I come to, an Englishman who gave me the anaesthetic said: "You know you're a lucky boy?" I said: "How do you make that out?" He said if you had gone over there [to the British operating theatre] they would've taken your leg off. It would've been quicker for them to cut your leg off. [Instead the French surgeons] have scraped everything out – they haven't cut you at all.'

However, while he was having his leg saved by a French surgeon, what George did not know was that his mother was grieving over his loss. According to George, she had been sent a letter from his major on her birthday – 10 October – 'to say that I'd been killed. The wording on the letter was: "We must not grieve because he was killed outright."'

Following his operation in France, George and other wounded soldiers were taken across the Channel on the hospital ship *Western Australia*, and he ended up at the 3rd Western General Hospital in Cardiff. George said: 'My name came out in the *Echo*. It said: "Convoy of wounded come to Cardiff and there are only two Welshmen in the convoy – Edwards from Aberdare, and Richards from Cymer." We had neighbours two doors away from my mother. One of the daughters ran up

CANADIAN SOLDIERS OCCUPY THE STILL BURNING TOWN OF CAMBRAI, FOLLOWING ITS CAPTURE IN OCTOBER 1918, WHEN GEORGE RICHARDS WAS INJURED.

and said: "George is alive, George is alive." "Oh no my dear, he's not alive." "Yes, look, it's in the *Echo*." "No, I've had a letter from the major." After she came in and found it was me, she said "I was afraid to look in case it wasn't you."' George, an amateur artist, claimed that his stepfather had destroyed almost all the drawings and paintings he had ever made. However, the family believe that because his mother had thought George was dead, she found the pictures a constant reminder of what she had lost, and wanted them to be burned.

George was recuperating at a Red Cross hospital in Barry, near Cardiff, when the Armistice was announced. 'It was like a big weight had been lifted,' he said. Able-bodied patients held dances on the wards, by pushing the beds back up to the wall, and when they ventured into town for twice-weekly visits to the theatre, they were treated like heroes. 'One chap there, he had his leg off [yet] he was the life of the party,' said George. 'We used to carry him on a stretcher with a Union Jack over him and he had a tin whistle. We had the time of our lives and we were invited out to the nurses' homes.' However, as the soldiers were discharged, the amputee's attitude changed. 'He said: "It's all right now you're going back amongst pals – you can walk about freely. I'm going back now – I won't be able to." We tried to cheer him up the best way we could – he was probably broken hearted, but before that he was the life of the party. It could've happened to me. When I went out to France [i.e. later] I made sure that was my main intention ... to thank them for what they had done to me.'

George's son Gordon said his father never forgot how close he had been to losing a limb like his comrade at Barry hospital. 'Dad was immensely grateful to the French for saving his leg,' he said. 'He often remarked when he had a bit of a limp – "I should be thankful I still have my leg." And when he went back to France in the late 1980s for the unveiling of a memorial to the Battle of Mametz Wood, he made sure he thanked a Frenchman for the two surgeons that saved his life.' 5

George was finally discharged in February 1919, and his leg was sufficiently healed for him to return to work as a miner. He met and married Harriet Ellen Owen in Bridgend, South Wales, and the couple went on to have three sons – Walter, Gordon and Clifford. 'Dad was a pretty independent sort of bloke – very self reliant – and we three boys got the distinct impression that this was the sort of attitude he was trying to instil in us,' said Gordon. 'Because of his disappointment in his own education, he was absolutely insistent that we became as well qualified as we were able to be and we were given every encouragement. We all went to grammar school and university, and we all got degrees.' Gordon's brother, Clifford, said: 'Some veterans didn't talk about the war, but our father always talked about it, which I think was a good thing as it got it out of his system. It was fascinating for us boys listening to his stories – better than going to the pictures. But his experience firmly established his view on war.'

And George's final verdict on the 1914–18 conflict, as summed up by Clifford, would be shared by many people: 'He thought it was an appalling waste of life, and there were better ways to deal with a crisis than resorting to violence.'

Endnotes

1 Observation balloons were tethered aerial platforms used by both sides along the Western Front to gather intelligence and spot artillery. Observers would spend several hours in the air passing on information via semaphore, or occasionally by radio. If they came under attack or the balloons caught fire, observers would have to resort to their parachutes to escape.
2 'Mills bomb' – a type of grenade.
3 George's wound at Cambrai was recorded in his British Army medical report at the time. His medal card also reveals that he was a private in both the South Wales Borderers and the Welsh Regiment.
4 'Lewis gun' – a light machine gun (*see* Endnote 3, page 85).
5 The 38th (Welsh) Division captured Mametz Wood during the Battle of the Somme in July 1916. A red dragon memorial to the fallen was dedicated next to the wood in 1987. George Richards was among a number of veterans at the ceremony.

INDEX